POWER AND LIBERTY

POWER AND LIBERTY

Constitutionalism in the American Revolution

Gordon S. Wood

OXFORD
UNIVERSITY PRESS

OXFORD
UNIVERSITY PRESS

Oxford University Press is a department of the University of Oxford. It furthers
the University's objective of excellence in research, scholarship, and education
by publishing worldwide. Oxford is a registered trade mark of Oxford University
Press in the UK and certain other countries.

Published in the United States of America by Oxford University Press
198 Madison Avenue, New York, NY 10016, United States of America.

CIP data is on file at Library of Congress
ISBN 978-0-19-754691-8

DOI: 10.1093/oso/9780197546918.001.0001

1 3 5 7 9 8 6 4 2

Printed by Sheridan Books, Inc., United States of America

To Jack, Jim, Norman, and Tony
All of us practicing the art of growing older

CONTENTS

ACKNOWLEDGMENTS

This book began as a series of lectures that I presented at the Northwestern University Pritzker School of Law in the fall of 2019. I want to thank Dean Kimberly A. Yuracko and her colleagues for the invitation and for the splendid hospitality they showed my wife and me during our stay in Chicago. I especially want to extend my thanks to Professors Robert Bennett, Steven G. Calabresi, Andrew M. Koppleman, James T. Lindgrin, John O. McGinnis, and James E. Pfander for their many kindnesses. In addition to their hospitality, Professor Pfander ran the mini-course that I taught, and Professor Koppleman offered some astute advice on several lectures that he read. I have a special thanks to Glenn Weinstein and Lindsey Arenberg for the warm friendship they extended to my wife and me during our visit to Chicago; it was extraordinary, and we will never forget it.

My thanks too to Richard D. Brown, Patrick Conley, and Stanley Lemons for supplying some essential information. I also extend my thanks to the two anonymous reviewers who helped improve the manuscript, to copy editor Mary Anne Shahidi, and to Joellyn

Ausanka and Amy Whitmer, senior production editors at Oxford, who shepherded the manuscript through the production process. I am especially grateful for the editorial expertise of the indefatigable Susan Ferber. She is a special jewel in the crown of Oxford University Press. Finally, my thanks to Louise for everything.

POWER AND LIBERTY

Introduction

In his pamphlet *Common Sense,* published six months before the Declaration of Independence, Thomas Paine called for a "CONTINENTAL CONFERENCE," which, "being impowered by the people," would have the legal authority to draw up a "CHARTER," a written document for America "answering to what is called the Magna Charter of England." This charter would outline the form of government and secure "freedom and property to all men," especially the rights of conscience, and "such other matter as is necessary for a charter to contain." Then, said Paine, the Conference, which was not the government but an "intermediate body between the governed and the governors," would dissolve, its work of framing the charter done. The framers of such an enlightened government, a government, said Paine, that fixed "the true points of happiness and freedom," would "deserve the gratitude of ages." To those unenlightened conservatives who dare to ask, where is the king? tell them, "in America THE LAW IS KING."[1]

In this extraordinary passage from his extraordinary pamphlet, Paine anticipated much of the constitutional work carried out by the Revolutionary generation of Americans over the next three or four decades. Although Paine had arrived in America only in November 1774, he was emotionally and intellectually prepared to be an American. A former corset maker, schoolmaster, and twice-dismissed excise officer, the thirty-seven-year-old Paine had left England full of rage at the decadent monarchical society that had kept him down and by 1776 was ready to articulate America's destiny.

Because of his uncanny ability to extract from the culture the most progressive elements of enlightened thinking, Paine, a middling "mongrel," as John Adams called him, "begotten by a wild Boar on a bitch Wolf," was often able to be more American than those born and raised in the New World. Certainly, his emphasis on charters written at a moment in time and embodying, like Magna Carta, a fundamental law that protected individual liberties and rights was thoroughly American. Perhaps Adams was not entirely wrong when he sarcastically suggested that the Revolutionary era ought to be called "the Age of Paine."[2]

The Revolutionary era was the most creative period of constitutionalism in American history and one of the most creative in modern Western history. During the five or six decades between the early 1760s and the early nineteenth century, Americans debated and explored all aspects of politics and constitution-making—the nature of power and liberty, the differing ideas of representation, the importance of rights, the division of authority between different spheres of government or federalism, the doctrine of sovereignty, the limits of judicial authority, and the significance of written constitutions. There was scarcely an issue of politics and constitutionalism that eighteenth-century Americans didn't touch upon.

Rarely has any nation in such a short period of time discussed and analyzed so many different issues of constitutionalism and created and secured so many political institutions, institutions that have lasted for more than two hundred years. Perhaps fifth-century Athens had similar debates, but we don't know much of what the

Athenians said. Seventeenth-century England had important constitutional discussions, but we have only a fragment of what the English participants discussed.

The case of America's constitutional origins is different. We Americans have an enormous amount of material covering the half-century of discussions and debates concerning power, liberty, and constitution-making, much of it now available both online and in letterpress editions.

These debates and documents--and those who engaged in the debates and created the documents--have an immediacy, a present-day relevance for Americans, that is extraordinary. The principles embodied in these documents seem to have a quality that transcends time and space. Americans look back to the eighteenth-century revolutionaries and the constitutions and documents they wrote with a special awe and respect. *The Federalist* papers, for example, have assumed a quasi-sacred character. Although the papers were polemical pieces dashed off in defense of the new Constitution during the heated debate over its ratification in the state of New York, they are now regarded as authoritative sources for interpreting the Constitution, and as such are even cited by the justices of the Supreme Court. So important has *The Federalist* become that in 1980 a concordance of the papers was put together, so that, like the Bible, every word and every phrase in the eighty-five papers can be parsed and analyzed. No other major nation invokes its two-hundred-year-old founding documents and their authors and in quite the way America does.[3]

It is not simply our continual concern with constitutional jurisprudence and original intent that explains our fascination with the eighteenth-century founding and its debates and documents. More important for Americans, these founding documents and the principles expressed in them have become our source of identity.

The identities of other nations, say, being French or German, have become lost in the mists of time, and their nationhood, their sense of having a common ancestry, has usually been taken for granted (which is why such nations are having greater problems with immigrants than we are). But Americans have never been a nation in any traditional or ethnic meaning of the term. By the early nineteenth century John Adams wondered whether America could ever be a real nation. In the United States, he said, there was nothing like "the Patria of the Romans, the Fatherland of the Dutch, or the Patrie of the French." All he saw in America was an appalling diversity of religious denominations and ethnicities. In 1813 he counted nineteen different religious sects in the country. "We are such an Hotch potch of people," he lamented, "—such an omnium gatherum of English, Irish, German, Dutch, Sweedes, French, &c. that it is difficult to give a name to the Country, characteristic of the people."[4]

Lacking any semblance of a common ancestry, Americans have had to create their sense of nationhood out of the documents—the declarations and constitutions and bills of rights—and the principles embodied in them that accompanied their eighteenth-century Revolution. Because the United States had no ethnic basis for its nationhood, it was ideally suited to become a nation of immigrants, something Abraham Lincoln clearly recognized and celebrated. Half the population of the United States, he said on the eve of the Civil War, had no direct blood connection to the Revolutionary generation. Nevertheless, all these German, French, Irish, and Scandinavian immigrants who had come to America since the Revolution had, said Lincoln, found themselves "our equals in all things." The moral principles embodied in the Revolutionary documents, especially in the Declaration of Independence with its claim that all men are created equal, made, he said, all these different peoples one with the founders, "as though they were blood of the blood and flesh of the flesh of the men who wrote the Declaration," and by implication all the other great documents of the Revolutionary era. No wonder Americans make so much of their founders.[5]

The constitutional debates and discussions that produced all these documents went through several phases during the Revolutionary period. It began in the early 1760s with a debate between the British colonists and the politicians in the mother country of Great Britain over the nature of the empire. During this imperial debate, which is the subject of chapter 1, both the colonists and the English government were surprised to discover that their experience in the empire over a century and a half had drastically diverged. The colonists' idea of representation had developed very differently from that of the British. At the same time, the British had constructed a notion of parliamentary sovereignty that was at odds with the Americans' understanding of divided political power. The colonists desperately tried to convince the English of the need for recognizing separate spheres of authority in the empire, but to no avail. The British clung to Parliament as the bulwark of their liberties, forcing the colonists to escape from Parliament's authority entirely and to make their allegiance to the king the sole tie keeping them in the empire. The debate climaxed with the Declaration of Independence in 1776, probably the greatest document in American history.

With independence, the thirteen new republics drew up constitutions (the focus of chapter 2) in which the framers sought to implement what they had learned from the imperial debate and from their previous experience in the empire. In order to prevent the rise of tyranny in their societies, they severely limited gubernatorial or magisterial power in a variety of ways and at the same time expanded the liberty of their popular houses of representatives. Although most of the new republican governments retained a semblance of the mixed model of the English constitution—with executives, upper houses, and houses of representatives—they were seriously unbalanced, with an extraordinary amount of power granted to the greatly enlarged lower houses. These Revolutionary state constitutions set the basic pattern for America's governments over the next two and a half centuries, including the federal government. The national Constitution, created a decade after the Declaration of Independence, was derived largely from the state constitutions.

The thirteen independent states came together in a league of union based on a treaty, the Articles of Confederation, that was finally ratified in 1781, only two years before the end of the eight-year war with Great Britain. Although this confederation, resembling the present-day European Union, was as strong as any confederation in history, its Congress lacked the powers to tax and regulate trade. But the problems Americans faced in the 1780s, described in chapter 3, seemed to some to go well beyond the obvious inadequacies of the Articles. These problems had to do with the excesses of democracy in the states, supported by an emerging middle class. The state legislatures were running amuck, creating evils involving the mutability, multiplicity, and injustice of laws—all of which brought the Americans' experiment in republican government into question. Reformers concerned with the rampaging state legislatures were able to use the nearly unanimous desire to amend the Articles of Confederation as a cover for scrapping the Articles and creating an entirely new national government embodied in the Constitution of 1787.

James Madison, who more than anyone was responsible for the Convention that drew up the new federal Constitution, was frustrated by the fragmentary and inadequate record of previous constitution makers. He wanted to ensure that subsequent framers of constitutions would know how Americans in 1787 went about creating a new government. His determination to keep as many notes as possible on what was said in the Convention accounts for the extraordinary record we have of the debates, analyzed in chapter 4. In one modern printed edition Madison's notes cover more than 550 pages.[6] The Convention had been closed to the public, and Madison's notes were not published until 1840, several years after his death, criticism of the Convention's secrecy, including that by Thomas Jefferson, led to an agreement that the popular ratifying conventions in 1787–88 would be open to the public.

These debates within the conventions were accompanied by multitudes of writings and discussions out of doors, all creating an extraordinary record of opinions about politics and the proposed Constitution. Over the past half-century, editors at the Historical Society of Wisconsin have collected every scrap of evidence pertaining to these discussions surrounding the ratification of the Constitution and have published their collections in more than two dozen modern letterpress volumes, with more to come. The participants in these debates included not just the elite leaders, such as James Madison and Alexander Hamilton, but also dozens of middling men, such as William Findley of Pennsylvania and Melancton Smith of New York, together with numerous backbenchers whom no one today has heard of. There is nothing quite like this collection of debates over politics and constitutionalism in the early modern period anywhere in the world.

The breadth and depth of popular interest in the Constitution in 1787–88 was remarkable. The towns of Massachusetts, for example, elected 370 delegates to the state's ratifying convention, of whom 364 attended. Most were eager to meet and discuss the Constitution. It took six days for the delegates from Bath, Maine (then part of Massachusetts), to make their way south across rivers and through snow to Boston. The people of Massachusetts believed they were involved, as the little town of Oakham told its delegates, in deciding an issue of "the greatest importance that ever came before any Class of Men on this Earth." The town of Richmond in the far west of Massachusetts held four meetings in December 1787 at four different times and places to discuss the Constitution, and on Christmas Eve the town finally voted that it was "not proper to adopt the Constitution as it now stands." Interest in the Constitution was the same everywhere. Richmond, Virginia, the new capital of the state, had trouble accommodating not only the 170 delegates to the ratifying convention but also what one observer called the "prodigious number of People from all parts of the Country" who wanted to witness the debates.[7]

One of the major issues both in the Convention and in the ratification debates involved slavery—the subject of chapter 5. In 1787 the northern states were already moving against the institution, and even Virginians were taking steps that seemed to point toward the abolition of slavery. There was a widespread feeling in the North and even in the Upper South that slavery was dying a natural death, which helps account for the willingness of the delegate to the Convention to make some compromises with the slaveholding states.

Crucial for understanding the constitutionalism of the Revolutionary era is the emerging role of the judiciary, which is the topic of the sixth chapter. Although Alexander Hamilton in *The Federalist* called the judiciary the "weakest" branch of the new federal government, developments over the following two decades or so revealed its latent authority.[8] Some Americans came to believe that the courts at times were more capable than the elective branches in setting social policy. Perhaps nowhere else in the world do courts wield as much power in shaping the conditions of life as they do in the United States—and that judicial power first emerged in the Revolutionary era.

The Revolution became much more than a break from Great Britain and a war for independence. It released pent-up social forces in the North that turned northern society into a middle-class world. These Revolutionary social developments moved much of the country into modernity, as revealed by the emerging demarcation between public and private realms, the theme of chapter 7. No doubt the American Revolution has little in common with the violence and terror of the French Revolution, but the two revolutions do share this momentous separation of public and private spheres.

This book, which is largely a distillation of my fifty years of work on the subject, is in no way a complete history of constitutionalism in the Revolutionary era. There are so many more subjects to be explored and written about—the constitutional issues relating to the native peoples, for one obvious example. Although it may not cover all issues, in those it covers, it is not meant to be partial to any political view, and it is not seeking to retrieve a usable past.[9] Assuming that every nation needs its history to be as accurate as possible, this book aims to recover those aspects of America's constitutional history it deals with as impartially and as truthfully as possible. These are difficult times, and any claim of objectivity is immediately suspect. But without a commitment to objective truth and the pastness of the past, the history of a nation becomes distorted, turns into politics by other means, and ends up becoming out-and-out partisan propaganda. But as impartial as it seeks to be, this book makes no claim to possessing any final truth. Because the sources are so rich and the stakes are so high, interpreting and reinterpreting the constitutional history of the era of the founding will continue just as long as the republic endures.

Chapter 1

The Imperial Debate

The imperial debate between Great Britain and its colonies in North America was precipitated by the peace ending the Seven Years' War, or the French and Indian War, as the colonists called it. Britain emerged from the war as the greatest and richest empire since the fall of Rome. The Treaty of Paris of 1763 ending the war gave Britain undisputed dominance over the eastern half of North America. From the defeated Bourbon powers, France and Spain, Britain acquired huge chunks of territory in the New World—all of Canada, East and West Florida, and millions of fertile acres between the Appalachian Mountains and the Mississippi River. At the same time, France turned over to Spain New Orleans and the vast territory of Louisiana in compensation for Spain's loss of the Floridas. Thus France, the most fearsome of Britain's enemies, was entirely removed from the North American continent.

But these new territories were expensive to defend. British officials, knowing that their fellow subjects in the home island were already heavily taxed, naturally thought of extracting money from the colonists in North America. After all, the colonists had an unusually high standard of living, as British officers had noted during the Seven Years' War, and thus the British government concluded that the colonists should help meet the expenses of defending the new territorial acquisitions that especially benefited them. Hence, royal officials began in 1764 tightening up the customs service and turning the Molasses Act of 1733 into a revenue-raising measure with a Sugar Act. In the past the colonists had more or less avoided confronting the constitutionality of the Molasses Act by smuggling and bribery. And since they had accepted the Navigation Acts in the seventeenth century, they had not generally denied Parliament's authority to regulate their trade, which was what the Sugar Act seemed to be. Consequently, their constitutional protests against it were few and far between.

That was not the case a year later with the Stamp Act. In 1765 the British government decided to levy a stamp tax on colonial legal documents, bonds, deeds, almanacs, newspapers, college diplomas, and playing cards—indeed, on nearly every form of paper used in the colonies.[1]

Some of the colonial governments had used stamp duties on various occasions, but this was the first time the home government had levied this kind of direct tax on the colonists. Since the British government had borrowed heavily to fight the war and was deeply in debt, it seemed only right that the colonists should pay their fair share of the postwar expenses, many of which accrued from Britain's maintaining military forces in the newly acquired territories.

The colonists thought otherwise. The Stamp Act ignited a firestorm of opposition that swept through the colonies with unprecedented force. In each colony the stamp agents were mobbed and forced to resign. Except briefly in Georgia, none of the colonists ever paid any stamp taxes.

The Stamp Act sparked more than riots and mobs. As the first unmistakable tax levy by Parliament, the act immediately raised the colonists' objections to a high level of constitutional principle. It precipitated an immensely important constitutional debate between British officials and the colonists, involving many of the fundamental issues of politics and government. Once begun, this decade-long imperial debate escalated through several stages until it climaxed with the Americans' Declaration of Independence in 1776.

The argument was exhilarating and illuminating. It forced both the British and the colonists to bring to the surface and make sense of their differing experiences in the empire over the previous century—experiences that had largely been hidden from view. By the time the imperial debate was over, the Americans both had clarified their understanding of the nature of public power and at the same time had prepared the way for their grand experiment in republican self-government and constitution-making.

When the colonists learned of the Stamp Act, nine colonies sent thirty-seven delegates to a Congress that met in New York in October 1765. The Congress drew up a set of formal declarations and petitions denying Parliament's right to tax them. Being good Whigs and believing in liberty and its protector, Parliament, they were not ready to deny Parliament's authority entirely.

"It is inseparably essential to the freedom of a people, and the undoubted rights of Englishmen," the Stamp Act Congress declared, "that no taxes should be imposed on them, but with their own consent, given personally, or by their representatives." Since "the people of these colonies are not, and from their local circumstances, cannot be represented in the House of Commons in Great Britain," the Congress said, the colonists could only be represented and taxed by persons, chosen by themselves, in their respective provincial legislatures. This statement defined the American position at the outset of the controversy, and, despite much subsequent confusion and stumbling, this essential point was never shaken.[2]

Much of the confusion came from the Congress's acknowledgment at the opening of its declaration that the colonists owed "all due Subordination to that August Body the Parliament of Great Britain." Since Parliament had passed the Stamp Act, what did "all due Subordination" mean?[3]

Once the British government sensed a stirring of colonial opposition to the Stamp Act, a number of English pamphleteers set out to explain and justify Parliament's taxation of the colonies. The most important of these pamphlets was by Thomas Whately, the sub-minister under the prime minister George Grenville and the person who actually had drafted the Stamp Act.

Whately argued that the colonists, like Englishmen everywhere, were subject to acts of Parliament through a system of "virtual" representation. Even though the colonists, like "Nine-Tenths of the People of *Britain*," did not in fact choose any representatives to the House of Commons, they were, said Whately, undoubtedly "a Part, and an important Part of the Commons of *Great Britain*: they are represented in Parliament, in the same Manner as those Inhabitants of *Britain* are, who have no Voices in Elections."[4]

There were many people who did not actually vote in Britain but were nonetheless thought to be represented in the House of Commons. In fact, in 1765 the British electorate made up only a tiny proportion of the nation; probably only one in six British adult males had the right to vote. Still, that was a larger electorate than any place on the continent, which was why Britain prided itself on its House of Commons. There was nothing like it anywhere in Europe.

The colonies had an even broader electorate for their provincial assemblies, their miniature parliaments: as many as two out of three adult white males could vote. Certainly, this was not democratic by modern standards, since slaves and women and property-less white males could not vote, but it was certainly the largest percentage of voters of any people in the world at that time.[5]

In addition to its narrow electorate, Britain's electoral districts were a confusing mixture of sizes and shapes created over centuries of history. Some of the constituencies were large, with thousands of voters, but others were small and more or less in the pocket of a single great landowner. Many of the electoral districts had few voters, and some so-called rotten boroughs, like Old Sarum, had no inhabitants at all. The town of Dunwich continued to send representatives to the House of Commons, even though it had long ago slipped into the North Sea.

At the same time, some of England's largest cities, such as Manchester and Birmingham, which had grown suddenly in the mid-eighteenth century, had fifty thousand or more inhabitants, and yet sent no representatives to Parliament. The earlier medieval residence requirements for members of Parliament had long since fallen away, and members did not have to be residents of the districts they represented. That is still true in Britain today.

The British idea of virtual representation was a product of the peculiar circumstances of British history. This notion of being virtually represented struck Americans then, and us today, as absurd. It was an obvious violation of one person, one vote that we value. But it was not absurd for most Englishmen.

Whately and other Britons justified this hodgepodge of representation by claiming that people were represented in England *not* by the process of election, which was considered incidental to representation, but rather by the mutual interests that members of Parliament were presumed to share with all Englishmen for whom they spoke—including those, like the colonists, who did not actually vote for them.

Since the colonists did not vote for any members of Parliament, a few colonists, like Benjamin Franklin, sought to solve the problem by hesitantly suggesting that the Americans might be given one hundred seats in the House of Commons just as the Scots had been granted seats in Parliament by the Act of Union of 1707. But most colonists were adamantly opposed to any such representation in the House of Commons. They realized only too well that their distant representatives would be swamped by the English and Scottish MPs and easily manipulated by the ministry.

Instead, nearly all Americans immediately and strongly rejected the British claims that they were "virtually" represented in the same way that the nonvoters of cities like Manchester and Birmingham were. They pointed out that they did not elect anyone to Parliament.

In the most notable colonial pamphlet written in opposition to the Stamp Act, *Considerations on the Propriety of Imposing Taxes* (1765), Daniel Dulany of Maryland admitted the relevance in England of virtual representation, but he denied its applicability to the colonies. America, he said, was a distinct community from England and could not be virtually represented by the agents of another community. This was an ominous argument, since it suggested that the British and the Americans were already separate peoples.[6]

Others, such as John Joachim Zubly, a Swiss-born pastor from Georgia, pushed beyond Dulany's argument and challenged the very idea of virtual representation with what was called "actual" representation. If the people were to be properly represented in a legislature, Zubly said, not only did they have to actually vote for the members of the legislature, but they also had to be represented by members whose numbers were more or less proportionate to the size of the population they spoke for.[7]

For most Americans virtual representation made no sense at all. What purpose is served, asked James Otis of Massachusetts in 1765, by the continual attempts of Englishmen to justify the lack of American representation in Parliament by citing the examples of Manchester and Birmingham, which returned no members to the House of Commons? "If those now so considerable places are not represented," said Otis, "they ought to be."[8]

The idea of actual representation was a product of the colonists' history. Their electoral districts were not the products of developments that stretched back centuries, as they were in England. Rather, they were recent and regular creations that were related to obvious changes in population. When new towns in colonial Massachusetts were formed, two new representatives were usually sent to the General Court. The same was true in Virginia. When new counties were created, each sent two representatives to the House of Burgesses. In the 1760s there were actually rioting and mini-rebellions in the western counties of several colonies—in North and South Carolina and in Pennsylvania—because the westerners hadn't been extended representation in the provincial assemblies fast enough.

Because of their different experience, most Americans had come to believe in a very different kind of representation from that of their cousins in the mother country. Their belief in actual representation suggested that the process of election was not incidental to representation, but central to it. People actually had to vote for their representative in order to be represented.

The hidden unanticipated implications of this idea of actual representation were enormous. Assuming that the electoral process alone was the criterion of representation, it might become possible to believe that any official elected by the people, regardless of the nature of his office, would by the fact of election alone become a kind of agent of the people. Over the next two decades or so, this idea that the electoral process was the major measure of representation was drawn out in unexpected ways, eventually resulting in all parts of all American governments becoming in one way or another representatives of the people.

Since actual representation stressed the closest possible connection between the local electors and their representatives, it was only proper that representatives be residents of the localities they spoke for and that people of the locality have the right to instruct their representatives. Americans thought it only fair that localities be represented more or less in proportion to their population. Despite its shortcomings by today's standards, the Americans' eighteenth-century practice of actual representation was the fullest and most equal participation of the people in the processes of government that the modern world had ever known. Nowhere else in the world was the idea of popular consent taken so seriously.

Rather than dismissing the British view of virtual representation out of hand, we might try to appreciate some of its merits. Edmund Burke campaigning for election in 1773 summed up the idea of virtual representation in his famous speech to his Bristol constituents. He said Parliament was not "a *congress* of ambassadors from different and hostile interests, which interests each must maintain, as an agent and advocate, against other agents and advocates; but Parliament is a *deliberative* assembly of *one* nation, with *one* interest, that of the whole, where, not local purposes, not local prejudices ought to guide, but [only] the general good, resulting from the general reason of the whole."[9]

These are fine sentiments, but difficult to sustain in an electoral system organized by local districts. The US House of Representatives is often the congress of ambassadors that Burke warned against.

Local feelings are hard to ignore, as Burke discovered: he lost that Bristol election.

But there is another justification for virtual representation. With its opposite, actual representation, a person actually has to vote for the representative in order to be represented in the legislature. If that is true, does it mean that if the candidate a person didn't vote for wins the election, that that person is thereby not represented? What is the justification for majority rule? Why should minorities in the electorate accept rule by persons whom they didn't vote for? The concept of virtual representation answers these questions. It contends that the criterion of representation is based not on the process of election but instead on the mutuality of interests between the representative and the people at large; and thus it explains why people should obey the laws made by a representative whom they actually did not vote for. It explains why the minority accepts majority rule.

Benjamin Franklin was very much responsible for the next stage of the debate. In 1766 his testimony before the House of Commons (quickly published as a pamphlet) helped to justify Parliament's hasty and rather awkward repeal of the Stamp Act. To cover its embarrassing retreat, Parliament accompanied its repeal by passing in 1766 the Declaratory Act, which asserted its right to legislate for the colonies "in all cases whatsoever."[10]

This was a robust assertion of parliamentary sovereignty—that is, the doctrine that there had to be in every state one final, supreme, indivisible lawmaking authority, and in the British Empire that authority lay in Parliament. This doctrine of sovereignty, made famous by William Blackstone in his *Commentaries on the Laws of England* (1765) was the most powerful principle of government in eighteenth-century British political thought. Blackstone, like most eighteenth-century Englishmen, located sovereignty in Parliament, declaring "that what the parliament doth, no authority on earth can undo." This had ominous implications for the colonists facing an objectionable parliamentary statute. Blackstone went on to point out that there wasn't anything anyone outside of Parliament could do about it. "If the parliament will positively enact a thing to be done, which is unreasonable," he said, "I know of no power that can control it."[11] This belief in the sovereignty of Parliament was what made its quick repeal of the Stamp Act so humiliating and the need to follow the repeal with the Declaratory Act so essential. The proper location of sovereignty—this supreme lawmaking power—became the issue that finally broke up the empire.

Franklin in his testimony suggested that the colonists would always object to an "internal" tax like the stamp tax, because they were not represented in Parliament, but they might not object to an "external" duty on imports, since they had always recognized the right of Parliament to regulate the trade of the empire. In other words, the colonists from the seventeenth century had admitted that Parliament had some authority over them. In 1733 Parliament had levied duties on imported foreign molasses, but these were prohibitory duties designed to control the flow of trade, not to raise revenue. Franklin, living in London for a decade, was a pragmatic imperial official who knew that empires cost money, but he was a bit out of touch with American opinion. Maybe, he suggested, the British government could levy external duties on colonial imports and raise revenue that way.[12]

Although few colonists had made anything of this distinction between internal and external taxes, the British government grasped at it. In 1767 the chancellor of the exchequer, Charles Townshend, admitted that he could not see "any distinction between internal and external taxes; it is a distinction without a difference, it is perfect nonsense." But "since Americans were pleased to make that distinction," he said he was "willing to indulge them."[13] Consequently, Parliament went on to levy "external" taxes, or duties on colonial imports of lead, glass, paper, and tea, the revenue from which was to be applied to the salaries of royal officials in the colonies.

These Townshend Duties aroused instant opposition in the colonies. John Dickinson, a wealthy and influential Pennsylvania lawyer, attempted to sort out the limits of Parliament's authority, which the colonists were not yet willing to totally defy. His *Letters from a Pennsylvania Farmer* (a nice rhetorical strategy for a wealthy city lawyer to pose as a farmer) was the most popular pamphlet in the imperial debate until the appearance of Thomas Paine's *Common Sense*.

Dickinson, like nearly all colonists, conceded that Parliament had the right to regulate America's trade. After all, it had always done so since the Navigation Acts of the seventeenth century. But, wrote Dickinson, Parliament had no right whatsoever to tax the colonies, and it mattered not whether the taxes were internal or external.

But how to distinguish between duties designed to regulate trade and duties designed to raise revenue? The answer, said Dickinson, lay in the colonists' ability "to discover the intentions of those who rule over" us.[14] Suddenly, Americans had turned the imperial debate into an elaborate exercise in the deciphering of British motives— and this at a time when dissembling and deceit were thought to be everywhere in Anglo-American culture. It is not surprising that Americans became obsessed with conspiracies in the British government designed to deprive them of their liberties.[15]

By 1768 the colonists were still trying to explain their previous experience in the empire, admitting that Parliament had some authority over them, but not the authority to tax. In 1767 the New York legislature, for example, sought to declare which acts of Parliament were applicable in the colony and which were not.[16] Trying to draw these kinds of distinctions made them look confused.

So inconsistent and erratic did the colonists' positions seem that Allan Ramsey, a British Tory and the painter to the king, could only mock them. "One moment they desire no more than what belongs to every British subject," said Ramsay; "the next they refuse to be taxed like other British subjects." They admit they are under Parliament's authority, and yet "almost in the same breath" they claim that their petty assemblies were the equal of Parliament. They didn't seem to know their own mind. "At one time an American claims the rights of an Englishman; if these are not sufficient, he drops them, and claims the rights of an Irishman; and when these do not fully answer his purpose, he expects to be put upon the footing of a Hanoverian"— that is, a member of the electorate of Hanover whose head became George I in 1714.[17]

It was all too much for the British. The willingness of Americans to accede to parliamentary regulation of their trade but to deny Parliament's right to tax them made no sense to British officials; and they finally exploded in frustration. To counter all of the colonists' halting and fumbling efforts to divide parliamentary power, the British government offered a simple but powerful argument based on the doctrine of sovereignty—that there had to be in every state one final, supreme, indivisible, lawmaking authority. Otherwise the government would end up with that absurdity of an *imperium in imperio*, a power within a power. And in the British Empire that sovereignty could be located only in Parliament.

In 1769 the British government enlisted a sub-cabinet official, William Knox, to clarify matters for the colonists in his pamphlet *The Controversy Between Britain and Her Colonies Reviewed*. Knox set forth the idea of sovereignty with utter clarity. If the colonists accepted "one instance" of Parliament's authority, then, said Knox, they had to accept all of it. And if they denied Parliament's authority over the colonists "in any particular," then they must deny it in "all instances," and the union between Great Britain and the colonies would be dissolved. "There is no alternative," Knox concluded. The colonists were either totally under Parliament's authority, or they were totally outside it.[18]

Knox's choice of alternatives burst the debate wide open. The debate had begun with the issue of representation and taxes. Could the colonists be taxed if they were virtually but not actually represented in Parliament? After Knox's pamphlet appeared, the issue became: where did sovereignty lie? The struggle to answer this question ultimately destroyed the empire.

Knox and other British officials thought that argument about sovereignty was unanswerable. Since tyranny in British history had always come solely from the Crown, good Whigs like Knox (Whigs being those who favored Parliament and liberty, Tories being those who favored the Crown and prerogative power) found it inconceivable that anyone in his right mind would want to escape from Parliament's libertarian protection. After all, Parliament was the august author of the Habeas Corpus Act, the Petition of Right of 1628, and the Bill of Rights of 1689, and was the historical guardian of the people's property and the eternal defender of their liberties against the encroachments of the Crown.

For the colonists this was the most difficult point in the debate. They had vehemently denied that Parliament had any right to tax them. They said that no Englishman could have his property taken away without his consent, and since they were not and could never be represented in Parliament, that consent could be given only by their colonial legislatures. But at the same time, they had admitted that they owed all "due Subordination to that August Body, the Parliament of Great Britain."

John Dickinson had put his finger on the problem. In his *Letters from a Farmer in Pennsylvania* he had questioned the parliamentary act suspending the New York legislature for its failure to supply the British troops in accord with the Quartering Act. If the Crown had suspended the New York assembly, said Dickinson, that would have been an act of the king's prerogative and thus constitutional. As good Whigs, the colonists knew how to deal ideologically with any encroaching power of the Crown, but the power of Parliament was different. Using parliamentary legislation instead of the king's prerogative power to suspend the legislature, warned Dickinson, gave "the suspension a consequence vastly more affecting." If the members of Parliament could suspend the colony's legislature, they could effectively "lay *any burthens* they please upon us."[19]

It was left to Governor Thomas Hutchinson of Massachusetts to try to solve the problem and clarify for the colonists just what the sovereignty of Parliament meant. Hutchinson was a good Whig, and, like Knox, he could not imagine the colonists wanting to be outside of the authority of Parliament. Hutchinson, whose family dated back to the initial founding of the colony, was so confident of his position that he decided to lecture his fellow Massachusetts subjects in a formal manner and set them right on the nature of the English constitution.

In his speech to the two houses of the Massachusetts legislature, called the General Court, on January 6, 1773, Hutchinson extolled the English constitution for its spirit of liberty and lamented that some colonists in the province had seen fit over the previous decade to deny the authority of Parliament and subvert the constitution. Although he admitted that the English constitution allowed for subordinate powers, nonetheless there had to be "one supreme Authority over the whole," and that authority was Parliament. If the Council and House of Representatives had any doubts about that, he, like Knox earlier, invoked the doctrine of sovereignty to clinch his point.

"I know of no line," he declared, "that can be drawn between the supreme Authority of Parliament and the total Independence of the Colonies. It is impossible," he said, that "there should be two independent Legislatures in one and the same State, for although there may be but one Head, the King, yet the two Legislative Bodies will make two Governments as distinct as the Kingdom of England and Scotland before the Union."[20]

In its response the Council ignored the issue of sovereignty and, like the Stamp Act Congress in 1765, acknowledged Parliament's supremacy while at the same time claiming that its authority was not absolute. But the Massachusetts House of Representatives would have none of this equivocating. It faced Hutchinson's stark alternatives head-on and chose the one he never expected. "If there be no such Line [between the supreme authority of Parliament and the total independence of the colonies]," the House declared, "the Consequence is, either that the Colonies are the Vassals of Parliament, or, that they are totally Independent. As it cannot be supposed to have been the Intention of the Parties in the Compact, that we should be reduced to a State of Vassalage, the Conclusion is, that it was their Sense, that were thus Independent." Since, as Governor Hutchinson had said, having two independent legislatures in the same state was impossible, the colonies had to be "distinct States from the Mother Country," united and connected only through the king "in one Head and common Sovereign."[21]

In a lengthy speech on February 16, Governor Hutchinson attempted to rebut these responses, which prompted replies once again from the Council and the House. The House's reply, written by John Adams, was a long and detailed historical and legal justification of the colonists' claim of independence from Parliament and their connection to the empire only through the king.

On March 6, 1773, Hutchinson made one final effort to explain to his Massachusetts subjects the true nature of the English constitution, repeating once again that "in every Government there must be somewhere a supreme uncontrollable Power, an absolute Authority to decide and determine." By now most colonists in Massachusetts and elsewhere had come to agree with him; but for these colonists that "supreme uncontrollable power" was no longer Parliament.[22]

This marked an extraordinary moment in the history of the debate. By 1774 all of the leading patriot pamphlet writers—James Wilson, Benjamin Franklin, Thomas Jefferson, John Adams, and Alexander Hamilton—confronted with the same choice—being totally under Parliament's authority or totally outside of it—had chosen to cut themselves off completely from Parliament, but not from the British king.

All these leading colonists set forth a radically new conception of the empire. Each of the thirteen colonies, they contended, was completely independent of Parliament, but each retained an allegiance to the king as the common link in the empire.[23] James Wilson, for example, declared in 1774 that he entered upon the writing of his *Considerations on the Nature and Extent of the Legislative Authority of the British Parliament* with the "expectation of being able to trace some constitutional Line between those cases, in which we ought, and those in which we ought not, to acknowledge the power of Parliament over us." But in the process, Wilson, like many other Americans. "became fully convinced that such a Line does not exist; and that there can be no medium between *acknowledging* and *denying* that power in *all* cases." Only their allegiance to the king, which was not to be confused with representation, said Wilson, kept the colonies in the empire.[24]

Lord North, like other good Whigs in Britain, was baffled by the Americans' claim that they were totally outside of Parliament's libertarian protection and were instead tied solely to the king. Since the colonists were calling themselves Whigs, it didn't make sense to North any more than it did to Governor Hutchinson.

North thought he understood what the words Whig and Tory meant: that "it was," he said, "characteristic of Whiggism to gain as much for the people as possible, while the aim of Toryism was to increase the [king's] prerogative." By claiming that they belonged only to the king, the Americans, said North in 1775, were using the language of "Toryism."[25]

Historians have labeled the position Americans had reached by 1774 the "dominion theory" of the empire.[26] This label refers to the nature of the British Empire worked out in the Statute of Westminster of 1931. This statute created the modern British Commonwealth that established the legislative independence of each of the separate dominions, Canada, Australia, and New Zealand, which remain in the Commonwealth by their common allegiance to the British monarch.

By asserting their independence from the authority of Parliament, the colonists had not repudiated the doctrine of sovereignty. Quite the contrary: they had surrendered to it. Throughout a decade of debate, the colonists had tried over and over to divide legislative authority, saying that Parliament could do some things but not others. They sought desperately to get the British to acknowledge that there had to be separate spheres of authority in the empire. But the British, wedded to the principle of parliamentary sovereignty, could not admit any division of supreme authority.

By 1774 most of the patriot pamphleteers had given up. They despaired of trying to divide the indivisible, or separate the inseparable, and had finally accepted the logic of sovereignty—that there had to be in every state, as Blackstone had said, one final, supreme lawmaking authority. Two legislatures in the same state, concluded Alexander Hamilton in a common reckoning of 1774, "can not be supposed, without falling into that solecism of politics, of *imperium* in *imperio*." John Adams agreed. Two supreme authorities could not exist in the same state, he conceded in 1775, "any more than two supreme beings in one universe." Therefore, it was clear, he said, "that our provincial legislatures are the only supreme authorities in our colonies."[27]

The American colonists had disavowed the legislative authority of Parliament, but they had not disavowed the concept of legislative sovereignty; they had simply transplanted it to their miniature provincial parliaments, each of which now had a common head in the king.

But the problem of sovereignty did not go away. Ten years later the Anti-Federalists, the opponents of the new federal Constitution, raised the issue once again. They said that there had to be in every state only one final, supreme, indivisible lawmaking authority. Therefore, they said, because of the supremacy clause in the new federal Constitution, it was bound to be the federal government that would claim sovereignty. The states would eventually be reduced to trivial tasks, and the supreme authority would belong to the Congress. The defenders of the Constitution, the Federalists, as they called themselves, were faced with the problem of sovereignty all over again, and they had the same difficulty in trying to solve it as the colonists did in the 1770s.

Of course, by surrendering to the logic of sovereignty in 1774 and adopting this dominion theory of the empire, the colonists were not able to account for Parliament's previous and acknowledged regulation of their trade. Hence, by connecting themselves to the monarch alone, they had not offered a very satisfactory explanation of past experience in the empire. This was why James Wilson, a Philadelphia lawyer if ever there was one, was led to make his remarkable proposal in the final pages of his 1774 pamphlet to grant the king the prerogative power to regulate imperial trade, something, of course, the monarch at home had never possessed. That way the colonists could make sense of remaining in the empire with a connection only to the king—who would be able to use his prerogative power to make treaties that could regulate the empire's commerce.[28]

No one bought this unusual argument. The best that most colonists could do in 1774 was to allow Parliament to have power over their external commerce, as the Continental Congress awkwardly put it in 1774, "from the necessity of the case and a regard to the mutual interest of both countries"—not a very satisfactory solution to the problem.[29]

After 1774 the colonists tended to exclude Parliament from their arguments and increasingly focused on the king as the source of tyranny, a position that was much more in accord with their claim of being Whigs. It relieved the tension they had felt in taking on Parliament in the 1760s, the people's protector of liberty.

In his pamphlet of 1774, *A Summary View of the Rights of British Americans*, Thomas Jefferson prepared the way for the focus on the king. Since Jefferson, like other American leaders, had concluded that the colonists were not under Parliament's authority at all and were tied in the empire solely to the monarch, he tended to concentrate on the obnoxious actions of the king, a good conventional Whiggish position. In fact, his pamphlet was a dress rehearsal for the Declaration of Independence that he wrote two years later.

In his 1774 pamphlet Jefferson outlined a number of actions the English king had taken against the colonists. He charged that "for the most trifling reasons and sometimes for no conceivable reason at all, his majesty has rejected laws of the most salutary tendency." He even accused the king of preventing the colonists from abolishing the slave trade. But he didn't condemn the king outright; that would have been treasonous. Instead he declared that he was simply laying the colonists' grievances before his majesty. And he urged his majesty to open his breast to liberal and expanded thinking. "Let not the name of George the third be a blot in the pages of history." In a parting shot he claimed that kings were "the servants, not the proprietors of the people"—a claim that in the context of the eighteenth-century monarchical world was bold and revolutionary enough. It was by far the most radical pamphlet yet to appear.[30]

Up to 1775 the colonists had carried on their debate with Great Britain within the confines of the English constitution. The rights that the colonists claimed were the rights of Englishmen, the rights embodied in Magna Carta and other English documents. But to the members of the Continental Congress contemplating the possibility of independence, especially after war broke out in April 1775, it became awkward to talk continually of English rights. Thus they began more and more to refer to their rights as natural rights, rights that existed in nature and that did not have to be embodied in old parchments or musty records. Putting the rights on paper, they said, did not create them; it only affirmed their natural existence.

By January 1776 most American leaders were ready for Thomas Paine's *Common Sense*. Jefferson's questioning of the conduct of the king in his radical pamphlet was nothing compared to what Paine did in *Common Sense*. Paine took direct aim at hereditary monarchy in general and the British king in particular, and he did so in the most vulgar and insulting manner. He dismissed the institution of monarchy as absurd and called for American independence immediately. "For God's sake, let us come to a final separation . . . ," he implored. "The birthday of a new world is at hand."

Unlike John Dickinson and other pamphlet writers, Paine aimed his pamphlet directly at the unlearned and middling populace. He

consciously and deliberately rejected much of the traditional appa-
ratus of rhetoric and persuasion. He was determined to reach as wide
an audience as possible and to express feelings—revulsions and
visions—that the existing conventions of writing would not allow.
He looked for readers everywhere, but especially in the tavern- and
artisan-centered worlds of the cities. Consequently, he relied on his
readers knowing only the Bible and the English Book of Common
Prayer. He refused to decorate his work with Latin quotations and
scholarly references. Instead, he used simple, direct—some critics
said coarse, barnyard—metaphors. For example, he said that nature
obviously disapproved of monarchy; "otherwise she would not so
frequently turn it into ridicule, by giving mankind an *ass for a lion.*"

Few Americans had ever before read in print what Paine said
about kings and about George III, that "royal Brute of Britain"
who "made havoc of mankind." *Common Sense* went through two
dozen editions and sold at least 150,000 copies, at a time when
most pamphlets sold in the hundreds or a few thousand at best. The
same rate in today's US population would result in sales of more
than thirteen million copies. Although the pamphlet did not cause
Americans to think of declaring independence, it did express more
boldly and more clearly than any other writing what many of them
had come to feel about America's tie to the British Crown.

Paine saw that the Americans' protest against Great Britain had
become much more than an imperial spat over taxation. He told
Americans that they were involved in something more than a two-
bit colonial rebellion. They were participating in a world-shattering
historical event that had implications for all humanity. The contest
with Great Britain, he said, was not "the concern of a day, a year, or an
age," but of all time. And it concerned more than just the colonists.
The cause of America, he declared, is "the cause of all mankind."[31]

With the call for independence so dramatically expressed, it was just a matter of time before the Continental Congress took action. Because the colonists had concluded that they were not under Parliament's authority at all and were tied solely to the king, their Declaration of Independence needed to break only from the British monarch. Jefferson was released from all the restraints he may have felt in writing his earlier pamphlet. He could now unequivocally indict the king and blame him for every wrong. "He has refused . . . ," "He has forbidden . . . ," "He has plundered . . ." went each of the accusations against George III.

Since the colonists claimed they were never under Parliament's authority, they were anxious to play down Parliament's involvement in their oppression, even though Parliament had enacted the Stamp Act, the Townshend Duties, the Coercive Acts, and most of what the colonists had objected to in the decade since 1765.

Consequently, the Declaration scarcely mentioned Parliament. It did charge the king with combining "*with others* to subject us to a Jurisdiction foreign to our Constitution," and it conceded that they had warned their British brethren "from time to time of attempts by their legislature to extend an unwarrantable jurisdiction over us."[32] But that was it. By avoiding any great emphasis on Parliament, Jefferson and members of the Continental Congress, many of whom were lawyers, wanted their declaration to be scrupulously legal and in accord with the imperial relationship they had arrived at by 1774.

But the Declaration was more than a legal document; it became the most important document in American history. Its belief in natural rights that existed prior to government, which was established to secure those rights, and its claim that all men are created equal have resonated through all of American history. We are still debating their meaning.

Chapter 2

State Constitution-Making

We Americans are apt to think of the federal Constitution of 1787 as the model of constitutional thinking. It looms so large in our lives that we can scarcely pay any attention to our state constitutions. But the Revolutionary state constitutions created in 1776 were far more important in shaping America's understanding of constitutionalism than was the federal Constitution framed a decade later. Our single executives, our bicameral legislatures, our independent judiciaries, our idea of separation of powers, our bills of rights, and our unique use of constitutional conventions were all born in the state constitution-making period between 1775 and the early 1780s, well before the framing of the federal Constitution of 1787. In fact, the new federal government of 1787—its structure and form—was derived from what had taken place in the making of the state governments in the previous decade. In the first crucial years of independence, the states—not the federal government—were the focus of interest for most Americans.

Despite all the nationalizing and centralizing sentiments stirred up by the controversy with Great Britain in the 1760s and early 1770s, by the time of Independence a man's "country" was still his colony or state. Being a member of the British Empire had meant being an inhabitant of a particular colony with a history generally dating back a century or more. From these colonies the new states in 1776 inherited not only their geographical boundaries but also the affections and loyalties of their people.

The Declaration of Independence, though drawn up by the Continental Congress, was actually a declaration by "thirteen united States of America," proclaiming that as "Free and Independent States they have full Power to levy War, conclude Peace, contract Alliances, establish Commerce, and to do all other Acts and Things which independent States may of right do."[1]

In 1776 it was the states that were to be the arena for testing all that Americans had learned about politics both from their colonial experience and from the debate with Great Britain in the 1760s and 1770s. In fact, said Thomas Jefferson in the spring of 1776, making the new state constitutions was "the whole object of the present controversy."[2] The aim of the Revolution had become not merely independence from British tyranny, but nothing less than the eradication of the future possibility of tyranny.

Such a breathtaking goal explains the Revolutionaries' exhilaration in 1776 over the prospect of forming their new state governments. Because American leaders, as men of the Enlightenment, assumed that culture and institutions were man-made, framing their own governments became the ideal Enlightenment project. Americans believed, as John Jay of New York said, that they were "the first people whom heaven has favoured with an opportunity of deliberating upon, and choosing the forms of government under which they should live."[3]

Nothing in the years surrounding the Declaration of Independence—not the creation of the Articles of Confederation, not the making of the French alliance, and for some not even the military operations of the war—engaged the interests of the Americans more than the formation of their separate state governments. State constitution-making, said Jefferson, was "a work of the most interesting nature and such as every individual would wish to have his voice in."[4] Indeed, that seemed to be the case. Once independence was declared in July 1776, the business of the Continental Congress became stymied because so many delegates, including Jefferson, left Philadelphia for home to take part in the principal activity of erecting new state governments. Members of Congress, complained Francis Lightfoot Lee of Virginia, "go off & leave us too thin." For "alass [sic], Constitutions employ every pen."[5]

Some of the colonies, which were virtually independent by 1774, had already begun changing their governments. In the summer of 1775 Massachusetts had resumed its charter of 1691, which had been abrogated by the Coercive Acts. Since the royal governor was gone, the Council acted as the executive; but everyone knew that this situation was temporary. In the winter of 1775–76 New Hampshire and South Carolina also drew up temporary governments. But after the Declaration of Independence, constitution-making become more permanent.

These constitutions were written documents. Like Magna Carta, they could be picked up and read, quoted and analyzed. During the imperial debate the word *constitution* had been bandied about, used and abused in so many different ways, that Americans in 1776 realized that their constitutions had to be written down. The English constitution that the colonists had tried to appeal to was so vague, so intangible, that they knew that they had to have constitutions that were solid and secure.

By December 1776 eight of the revolutionary states had created new constitutions. Two states—Rhode Island and Connecticut, which as corporate colonies had elected their governors and were in fact already republics—revised their existing colonial charters by simply eliminating all references to the Crown. Delayed by wartime exigencies, two more states—Georgia and New York—wrote constitutions in 1777. In 1778 South Carolina drew up a more permanent constitution that did away with the governor's veto power and brought it more in line with the other revolutionary state constitutions. Massachusetts was not able to complete an acceptable constitution until 1780, and New Hampshire followed in 1784.

All in all, it was an extraordinary achievement. Never in history had there been such a remarkable burst of constitution-making. It captured the attention of intellectuals everywhere in the world. The state constitutions were soon translated into several European languages and published and republished and endlessly debated by European intellectuals. It was to refute French criticism of the state constitutions for being too much like the English constitution that John Adams wrote his three-volume master work, *Defence of the Constitutions of Government of the United States of America* (1787–88).

Adams had a vested interest in the state constitutions, for no one had been more important than he in influencing the structure and form of the new republics. Although Americans knew that their new governments would be republics, which presumably meant that they would contain no hereditary elements, they were not sure what precise form they would take. "Of Republics," said Adams in his significant pamphlet *Thoughts on Government*, published in April 1776, "there is an inexhaustible variety, because the possible combinations of the powers of society, are capable of innumerable variation." By *powers of society*, Adams meant what Europeans called estates—in his case, monarchy, aristocracy, and democracy, or the one, the few, and the many.[6]

Paine in his pamphlet had suggested that America's new republican governments should contain only single houses of representatives. In other words, they would be democracies, according to the political science of the day. This suggestion infuriated John Adams. He told Paine that his plan of government was "so democratical, without any restraint or even an Attempt at any Equilibrium or Counterpoise, that it must produce confusion and every Evil Work."[7] Although Paine's suggestion influenced the unicameral legislature of the Pennsylvania constitution of 1776, which came as close to a representative democracy as was possible for a large state in the eighteenth century, most of Adams's fellow Americans followed Adams's advice and created mixed constitutions with houses of representatives, upper houses or senates, and single executives. Having governors, upper houses, and houses of representatives was much more in line with the governments they were used to.

In these new republican constitutions, the Revolutionaries' central aim was to prevent power, which they identified with the governors, from encroaching on liberty, which was the possession of the people or their representatives in the lower houses of the legislatures. Most sought to create some sort of mixture or balance between power and liberty, rulers and ruled—the kind of balance that typified the ideal English constitution.

In all the constitutions, the power of the much-feared governors or chief magistrates was severely diluted, while the power of the popular assemblies or houses of representatives was significantly increased, as was their membership. The colonial assemblies had been small: New York's house of representatives had twenty-eight members; New Jersey's, twenty; Maryland's, sixty; and New Hampshire's, thirty-five. The new state constitutions greatly enlarged the houses of representatives, doubling and sometimes quadrupling them in size, and made all of them annually elected, which was an innovation outside of New England.

The constitution-makers emphasized the actual representation and the explicitness of consent that had been so much a part of the imperial debate. In addition to requiring annual elections, they created more equal electoral districts, enlarged the suffrage, imposed residential requirements for both electors and the elected, and granted constituents the right to instruct their representatives. Five states stated that population ought to be the basis of representation, and wrote into their constitutions specific plans for periodic adjustments of their representation, so that, as the New York constitution of 1777 declared, the representation "shall for ever remain proportionate and adequate."[8] In the English-speaking world this was an extraordinary innovation, something the British did not achieve until several decades into the next century.

As a balancing force between these governors and the popular assemblies, upper houses or senates (the term taken from Roman antiquity) were created in all the states except Pennsylvania, Georgia, and Vermont. These senates were designed to embody the aristocracy set between the monarchical and democratic elements of these republicanized mixed constitutions. The senates were composed not of a legally defined nobility, but, it was hoped, of the wisest and best members of the society who would revise and correct the well-intentioned but often careless measures of the people, exclusively represented in the states' houses of representatives. These senates, although elected by the people in several states, had no constituents and were not at this point considered to be in any way representative of the people.

Of course, it was not long before some Americans began to question the aristocratic character of these senates. When reformers in the late 1770s suggested adding an upper house to Pennsylvania's unicameral legislature, they were accused of trying to foist a House of Lords on the state. The reformers defensively replied that that

was not at all their intention. All they wanted was "a double representation of the people."[9]

This reply had momentous implications. If the people could be
represented twice, why not three, four, or more times? By 1780 the
convention creating the Massachusetts constitution of 1780 drew
out these implications: it concluded that "the Governor is emphatically the Representative of the whole People, being chosen not by
one Town or County, but by the People at large."[10]

By assuming that the electoral process was the criterion of representation, Americans prepared the way for an extraordinary expansion of the idea of representation. If governors elected by the people
were thereby representatives of the people, then all elected officials
could be viewed as representatives of the people. Once Americans
began thinking like this, then it would not be long before some of
them began describing their republics as actually democracies—
since all parts of the mixed government, and not just the houses of
representatives (the democratic part of a mixed government), were
presumably representative of the people.

Because the constitution-makers in 1776, like good Whigs,
identified tyranny with magisterial authority, they were determined to fundamentally transform the role of the governors in
the new constitutions. This was one of the most momentous and
radical steps Americans of 1776 intended to take. The American
constitution-makers, unlike the English in 1215 and 1689, were not
content merely to erect higher barriers against encroaching power or
to formulate new and more explicit charters of the people's liberties.
In their ambitious desire to root out tyranny once and for all, they
went way beyond anything the English had attempted with Magna
Carta in 1215 or the Bill of Rights in 1689. They aimed to make
the gubernatorial magistrate a new kind of creature, a very pale reflection indeed of its regal ancestor. They wanted to eliminate the

magistracy's chief responsibility for ruling the society—a remarkable and abrupt departure from the English constitutional tradition. However much the English had tried periodically to circumscribe the Crown's power, they had not usually denied (except for the brief Interregnum of the seventeenth century) the Crown's principal responsibility for governing the realm. Indeed, it is the monarch and her ministers who formally and constitutionally still govern England.

Americans in 1776 wanted a very different kind of chief magistrate. Most agreed with William Hooper of North Carolina that "for the sake of Execution we must have a Magistrate," but it must be a magistrate "solely executive," a governor, as Thomas Jefferson's 1776 draft for the Virginia constitution stated, without a voice in legislation, without any control over the meeting of the assembly, without the authority to declare war and make peace, raise armies, coin money, erect courts, lay embargoes, or pardon crimes; in sum, they wanted a ruler, as John Adams proposed, "stripped of most of those badges of domination, called prerogatives"—prerogatives being those often vague and discretionary powers that royal authority had possessed in order to carry out its responsibility for governing the society.[11] As the Revolutionary war years would quickly show, such an enfeebled governor could no longer be an independent magistrate with an inherent right to rule but could only be, as Jefferson correctly called him, an "Administrator."[12]

The Pennsylvania constitution, the most radical of all the new state constitutions, eliminated even the office of governor. Instead, it granted executive authority to a twelve-man executive council directly elected by the people. Other states, while clinging to the idea of a single executive magistrate, in effect destroyed the substance of an independent ruler. The framers surrounded all the governors with controlling councils elected by the legislatures. And they provided for the annual election of nearly all the governors, gener-ally by the legislatures, limited the times they could be re-elected, and subjected them to impeachment.[13] So feared was magisterial power that the Georgia constitution required the annually elected governor to swear an oath that he would step down "peaceably and quietly" when his term had expired.[14] Perhaps this was not an unfounded fear, as demonstrated in our own time by numerous so-called "republican" rulers throughout the world refusing to sur-render their offices even when defeated in an election.

The powers and prerogatives taken from the governors were given to the legislatures, marking a revolutionary shift in the tradi-tional responsibility of government. Throughout English history, government had been identified exclusively with the Crown or the executive; Parliament's responsibility had generally been confined to voting taxes, protecting the people's liberties, and passing cor-rective and exceptional legislation. However, the new American state legislatures, in particular the lower houses of representatives, were no longer to be merely adjuncts of or checks on magisterial power; they were to assume familiar magisterial prerogatives, in-cluding the making of foreign alliances and the granting of pardons, responsibilities that seem inherently executive.

The transfer of nearly all political authority to the people's representatives in the lower houses of the legislatures led some Americans, like Richard Henry Lee of Virginia, to note that their new governments were "very much of a democratic kind," although "a Governor and a second branch of legislation are admitted."[15] In 1776 many still thought of democracy as a technical term of polit-ical science referring to rule by the people exclusively in the lower houses of representatives.

Since English kings and royal governors had maintained their power by abusing the filling of offices in order to "influence" or "corrupt" the Parliament and the colonial legislatures, the constitution-makers were especially frightened of the magisterial power of appointment. This power, they thought, was the main source of modern tyranny and the way in which George III had corrupted Parliament to bend it to his will. Hence, in the new constitutions they wrested the power of appointment from the traditional hands of the chief magistrate and gave it to the legislatures. No longer would the governors have the power to influence legislators and judges by appointing them to offices in the executive.

Four of the state constitutions justified this radical barring of dual officeholding by the principle of separation of powers, a doctrine made famous by Charles-Louis de Secondat, Baron de Montesquieu, in the middle of the eighteenth century. This separation of the executive, legislative, and judicial powers had a much more limited meaning in 1776 than it would later acquire in American constitutionalism. The constitution-makers invoked Montesquieu's doctrine not to limit the legislatures but rather to isolate the legislatures and the judiciaries from the kind of executive manipulation or "corruption" of the members of Parliament that characterized the English constitution. Thus, the revolutionary state constitutions, unlike the English constitution, categorically barred all executive and judicial officeholders from simultaneously sitting in the legislatures.

In their efforts to prevent the popular representatives and the senators from becoming the tools of an insidious gubernatorial power, an effort echoed in Article I, Section 6, of the federal Constitution, the state constitution-makers prohibited the development of parliamentary cabinet government in America, presumably forever. In America no one can be both a member of the legislature and a member of the executive at the same time.

As the British stumbled into their system of ministerial responsibility and modern cabinet government in the late eighteenth and early nineteenth centuries, America's constitutional development moved in an entirely different direction. Whereas the British require their ministers to be members of Parliament—indeed, it is the key to their system—we demand that the executive's cabinet officials be absolutely banned from sitting in the legislatures. That is what Americans in 1776 meant by separation of powers.

This was one of the two important ways in which the American and English constitutional systems came to differ during the American Revolution. The other was over the meaning of a constitution.

The American Revolutionaries virtually established the modern idea of a written constitution. Of course, there had been written constitutions before in Western history, but the Americans did something new and different. They made written constitutions a practical and everyday part of governmental life. They showed the world how written constitutions could be made truly fundamental and distinguishable from ordinary legislation and how such constitutions could be interpreted on a regular basis and altered when necessary. Further, they offered the world concrete and usable governmental institutions for carrying out these constitutional tasks.

Before the era of the American Revolution a constitution was rarely ever distinguished from the government and its operations. In traditional English thinking a constitution referred not only to fundamental rights but also to the way the government was put together or constituted. "By constitution," wrote Lord Bolingbroke in 1733, "we mean, whenever we speak with propriety and exactness, that assemblage of laws, institutions and customs, derived from certain fixed principles of reason, directed to certain fixed objects of public good, that compose the general system, according to which the community hath agreed to be governed."[16]

The English constitution, in other words, included fundamental principles and rights together with the existing arrangement of governmental laws, customs, and institutions. While it contained some written documents, it was not, as Supreme Court Justice William Paterson pointed out in 1795, "reduced to written certainty and precision" and embodied in a single document. "In England," said Paterson, "there is no written constitution, no fundamental law, nothing visible, nothing real, nothing certain." The English constitution lay "entirely at the mercy of the parliament." But in America, declared Paterson, "the case is widely different. Every State in the Union has its constitution reduced to written exactitude and precision."[17]

By the end of the Revolutionary era Americans had come to view a constitution as no part of the government at all. It was a written document distinct from and superior to all the operations of government. It was, as Thomas Paine said in 1791, "a thing antecedent to a government, and a government is only the creature of a constitution." And, said Paine, it was "not a thing in name only; but in fact." For Americans a constitution was like a bble, possessed by every family and every member of government. "It is the body of elements," said Paine, "to which you can refer, and quote article by article; and which contains . . . everything that relates to the complete organization of a civil government, and the principles on which it shall act, and by which it shall be bound."[18]

A constitution thus could never be an act of a legislature or of a government; it had to be the act of the people themselves, declared James Wilson in 1790, one of the principal framers of the federal Constitution of 1787. "In their hands it is as clay in the hands of a potter: they have the right to mould, to preserve, to improve, to refine, and to finish it as they please." If the English thought this new idea of a constitution resembled, as the English writer Arthur Young caustically suggested in 1792, "a pudding made by a recipe," the Americans were convinced that the English had no constitution at all.[19]

It was a momentous transformation of meaning in a short period of time. Like the other changes Americans made in their political culture during the revolutionary era, their new understanding of constitutionalism emerged initially out of their controversy with Great Britain.

Like all Englishmen, the eighteenth-century colonists had usually thought of power as adhering in the Crown and its prerogatives—that power always posing a potential threat to the people's liberties. Time and again they had been forced to defend their liberties against the intrusions of royal authority, usually expressed by the agents of the Crown, their royal governors. They relied for the defense of their liberties on their colonial assemblies and invoked their rights as Englishmen and what they called their ancient charters as barriers against crown power.

In the seventeenth century many of the colonies had been established by crown charters, corporate or propriety grants made by the king to groups like the Massachusetts Puritans or to individuals like William Penn and Lord Baltimore to found colonies in the New World. In subsequent years these written charters gradually lost their original purpose in the eyes of the colonists and took on a new importance, both as prescriptions for government and as devices guaranteeing the rights of the people against their royal governors. In fact, the whole of the colonial past was littered with such charters and other written documents of various sorts to which the colonial assemblies had repeatedly appealed in their squabbles with royal power.

In appealing to written documents as confirmations of their liberties, the colonists acted no differently from other Englishmen. From almost the beginning of their history, Englishmen had continually invoked written documents and charters in defense of their rights against the Crown's power. "Anxious to preserve and transmit" their liberties "unimpaired to posterity," the English people, observed one colonist in 1775, had repeatedly "caused them to be reduced to writing, and in the most solemn manner to be recognized, ratified and confirmed,' first by King John [with Magna Carta], then by his son Henry IIId . . . and again by Edward the 1st, to Hen. 4th . . . [and] 'afterwards by a multitude of corroborating acts, reckoned in all, by Lord Cook, to be thirty-two, from Edw. 1st to Hen. 4th and since, in a great variety of instances, by the bills of rights and acts of settlement.' All of these documents, from Magna Carta to the Bill of Rights of 1689 and the Act of Settlement of 1701, were merely written evidence of those "fixed principles of reason" from which Bolingbroke had said the English constitution was derived.[20]

Although eighteenth-century Englishmen talked about the fixed principles and the fundamental law of the constitution, most agreed that Parliament, as the representative of the nobles and people and as the sovereign lawmaking body of the nation, had to be the supreme guarantor and interpreter of these fixed principles of fundamental law. In other words, the English constitution did not limit Parliament in any way. In fact, Parliament was a creator of the constitution and the defender of the people's liberties against the Crown's encroachments; it alone protected and confirmed the people's rights. The Petition of Right, the act of Habeas Corpus, and the Bill of Rights of 1689 were all acts of Parliament, mere statutes not different in form from other laws passed by Parliament.

For Englishmen therefore, as the great eighteenth-century jurist William Blackstone pointed out, there could be no distinction between the "constitution or frame or government" and "the system of laws." All were of a piece: every act of Parliament was part of the English constitution and all law, customary and statute, was thus constitutional. "Therefore," concluded British theorist William Paley, "the terms *constitutional* and *unconstitutional*, mean *legal* and *illegal*."[21]

Nothing could be more strikingly different from what Americans came to believe. As early as 1773 John Adams realized that "many people had different ideas from the words *legally* and *constitutionally*." The king and Parliament, he said, could do many things that were considered legal but were in fact unconstitutional. The problem was how to distinguish one from the other. The American constitutional tradition diverged at the Revolution from the British constitutional tradition on just this point: on its capacity to distinguish between what was "legal" and what was "constitutional."[22]

The imperial debate had prepared Americans to think about political power differently from their cousins in Great Britain. During that debate in the 1760s and early '70s, the colonists came to realize that although acts of Parliament, like the Stamp Act of 1765, might be legal—that is, in accord with the acceptable way of making law—such acts could not thereby be automatically considered constitutional—that is, in accord with the basic rights and principles of justice that made the English constitution the palladium of liberty that it was. It was true that the English Bill of Rights of 1689 and the Act of Settlement in 1701 were only statutes of Parliament, but surely, the colonists insisted in astonishment, they were of "a nature more sacred than those which established a turnpike road." Consequently, the colonists began talking about some English statutes being "unconstitutional," a seemingly new and mystical word in British culture.[23]

Under this pressure of events the Americans gradually came to believe that the fundamental principles of the English constitution had to be lifted out of the lawmaking and other processes and institutions of government and set above them. "In all free States, the Constitution is fixed," declared the Massachusetts Circular Letter of 1768 (written by Samuel Adams), "and as the supreme Legislature derives its Powers and Authority from the Constitution, it cannot overleap the Bounds of it without destroying its own foundation."[24] Most eighteenth-century Englishmen would have found such a statement not just confusing but virtually incomprehensible.

A year later, in 1769, the Rev. John Joachim Zubly of Georgia clarified the Americans' point more fully. Britain had a Parliament which admittedly was the supreme legislature over the whole British Empire, but, said, Zubly, Britain also had a constitution. The Parliament "derives its authority and power from the constitution, and not the constitution from the Parliament." Surely the English nation, for example, would never consider a parliamentary law as constitutional that made the king's power absolute. Zubly concluded, therefore, "that the power of Parliament, and of every branch of it, has its bounds assigned by the constitution."[25]

Thus in 1776, when Americans came to frame their own constitutions for their newly independent states, they knew they had to be different from ordinary laws. They were determined to write them out explicitly in documents and somehow or other make them fundamental.

It was one thing, however, to define the constitution as fundamental law, different from ordinary legislation and circumscribing the institutions of government; it was quite another to make such a distinction effective. The distinction between fundamental and ordinary law was there for all to see, but everywhere there was confusion over how the fundamental law was to be produced and maintained. What institution or authority could create it? Could it still be fundamental if the legislatures created and altered it?

Consequently, many of the states in 1776 stumbled and fumbled in their efforts to make their constitutions fundamental.[26] Virginia simply declared that its constitution was fundamental. Delaware stated that its constitution was law and that some parts of that law were unalterable by the legislature. New Jersey allowed the legislature to change its constitution except for certain articles—those having to do with the right to trial by jury and the rules governing the legislature's composition, term of office, and powers.

Five of the states in 1776—Virginia, Pennsylvania, Maryland, Delaware, and North Carolina—prefaced their constitutions with bills of rights, combining in a jarring but exciting manner ringing declarations of universal principles with motley collections of common law procedures. Yet it was not always clear whether these bills of rights were fences just against the chief magistracy or against all the institutions of government, including the representatives of the people. Many in 1776 still thought that the legislatures representing the people ought to be capable, like Parliament, of altering the constitutions. In other words, they hadn't yet come fully to terms with the idea of a constitution as fixed and superior to ordinary legislation.

In 1776 most of the revolutionary state constitutions were written by provincial congresses or conventions acting in place of the legislatures, which the royal governors had dismissed or refused to convene. Thus, many constitution-makers initially assumed that because of the absence of the governors, their revolutionary conventions were legally deficient bodies, necessary expedients perhaps but not constitutionally equal to the formal legislatures in which the governors were present.

In 1688 the English, in the absence of James II who had fled to France, had relied on such a convention of the Lords and Commons to set forth a declaration of rights and to invite William and Mary to assume the vacant English Crown. But once the monarch was present, the convention immediately became a legitimate Parliament and the declaration of rights was reenacted as the Bill of Rights of 1689. In 1776 some of the American constitution-makers likewise felt uneasy about the fact that their constitutions had been created by mere conventions whose legality was suspect. The new state of Vermont felt so uneasy over the origins of its 1777 constitution by a mere convention that its legislature reenacted it in 1779 and again in 1782 "in order to prevent disputes respecting [its] legal force."[27]

At the same time, Americans struggled with ways of changing or amending their fundamental laws. All sensed to one degree or another that their constitutions were a special kind of law, but how to change it? Could a simple act of the legislature change the constitution? Delaware provided that five-sevenths of the assembly and seven members of the upper house could change those parts of the constitution that were alterable. Maryland said that its constitution could be changed only by a two-thirds vote of two successive separately elected assemblies. Pennsylvania pulled a monster out of Roman history, a council of censors, as a separately elected body to look into the constitution every seven years and if changes were needed, to call a special convention to revise it. So it went in state after state, as American groped their way toward the modern idea of a constitution as a fixed fundamental law superior to ordinary legislation.

Although Americans were convinced that constitutions were decidedly different from legislation, the distinction was not easy to maintain. They hadn't yet imagined what a constitution meant. They were conscious that their constitutions were written documents, but they weren't yet ready to define these constitutions simply by their fixed textuality. In other words, they still retained something of the older notion of a constitution as a dynamic combination of powers and principles. In the years following the Declaration of Independence many Americans paid lip service to the fundamental character of their state constitutions, but, like eighteenth-century Britons, they continued to believe that their legislatures were the best instruments for interpreting and changing these constitutions. After all, statutes of Parliament changed the common law and were integral parts of the English constitution. So the American state legislatures, which represented the people more equally than the House of Commons represented the British people, should be able to amend and change their state constitutions.

Thus, in the late 1770s and the early 1780s several state legislatures, acting on behalf of the people, set aside parts of their constitutions by statute and interpreted and altered them, as one American observed, "upon any Occasion to serve a purpose."[28] Time and again the legislatures interfered with the governors' legitimate powers, rejected judicial decisions, disregarded individual liberties and property rights, and in general, as one victim complained, violated "those fundamental principles which first induced men to come into civil compact."[29]

No one wrestled more persistently with the problem of distinguishing between statutory and fundamental law than Thomas Jefferson. Although he was anxious in 1776 to ensure the fundamental character of the new Virginia constitution, all he could suggest in his first draft of a constitution that the constitution be unrepealable except "by the unanimous consent of both legislative houses." By his second and third drafts, however, he had refined his thinking and proposed that the constitution be referred "to the people to be assembled in their respective counties and that the suffrages of two-thirds of the counties shall be requisite to establish it." This would make the constitution unalterable "but by the personal consent of the people on summons to meet in their respective counties."[30]

Jefferson soon recognized that his suggestions for making the constitution fundamental were too complicated. By 1779 he had also come to appreciate from experience that a constitution or any act that should be fundamental enacted by a legislature could never be immune to subsequent legislative meddling and altering. Assemblies, he said, "elected by the people for the ordinary purposes of legislation only, have no power to restrain the acts of succeeding Assemblies." Thus he realized that to declare his great act for Establishing Religious Freedom in Virginia to be "irrevocable would be of no effect in law; yet we are free," he wrote into the bill in frustration, "to declare, and do declare, that the rights hereby asserted are of the natural rights of mankind, and that if any act shall be hereafter passed to repeal the present or to narrow its operation, such act will be an infringement of natural right." In other words, all he could do in 1779 to make his act of religious freedom fundamental was to put a curse on subsequent lawmakers who might violate or tamper with it.[31]

Such a paper curse was obviously not enough, and Jefferson soon realized that something more was needed to protect basic rights and fundamental constitutions from legislative tampering. By the mid-1780s both he and James Madison were eager "to form a real constitution" for Virginia; the existing one enacted in 1776, they thought, was merely an "ordinance" with no higher authority than the other ordinances of the same session. They wanted a constitution that would be "perpetual" and "unalterable by other

legislatures." But how? If the constitution were to be truly fundamental and immune from legislative tampering, somehow or other
it would have to be created, as Jefferson put it, "by a power superior
to that of the legislature."[32]

By the time Jefferson came to write his *Notes on the State of
Virginia* in the early 1780s, the answer had become clear. "To render
a form of government unalterable by ordinary acts of assembly," said
Jefferson, "the people must delegate persons with special powers.
They have accordingly chosen special conventions to form and fix
their governments."[33]

In 1775–77, Americans had regarded their conventions or
congresses as legally deficient bodies made necessary by the refusal
of the royal governors to call together the regular and legal representatives of the people. By the 1780s, however, Jefferson and others
described these once legally defective conventions as special alternative representations of the people temporarily given the exclusive
authority to frame or amend constitutions.

Massachusetts in framing its constitution of 1780 had shown
the way, followed by New Hampshire in 1784. As Boston warned
its representatives in the legislature in 1778, they and their fellow
legislators could not create a constitution, for they may "form the
Government with peculiar Reference to themselves." Only a special constitution-making convention called "for this, and *this alone,*
whose Existence is known No Longer than the Constitution is
forming" could legitimately create a constitution.[34] Thus the General
Court in 1779 authorized the election of a special convention with
the sole duty of drafting a constitution, which then was to be sent
to the towns for ratification by two-thirds of the state's free adult
population. This Massachusetts experience set the proper pattern of
constitution-making and constitution-altering: constitutions were

created or changed by specially elected conventions and then placed before the people for ratification.

Therefore, in 1787 those who wished to change the federal government knew precisely what to do: they called a convention in Philadelphia and sent the resultant document to the states for approval by specially elected ratifying conventions. Even the French in their own revolution several years later followed the American pattern. Conventions and the process of ratification made the people the actual constituent power.

These were extraordinary contributions that Americans of the Revolutionary era made to the world—the practice of separation of powers, the modern idea of a constitution as a written document, the device of specially elected conventions for creating and amending constitutions, and the process of popular ratification.

It may be that the sources of these constitutional achievements lay deep in Western history. For centuries people had talked about fundamental law and placing limits on the operations of government. But not until the American Revolution had anyone ever developed such practical, everyday institutions not only for controlling government and protecting the rights of individuals but also for changing the very framework by which government operated. And all these remarkable achievements were realized prior to the formation of the federal Constitution—in the ten short years or so following the Declaration of Independence. Indeed, the creation of the federal Constitution in 1787 would not have been possible without the previous experience with state constitution-making. For many Americans in the decades following the Declaration of Independence, the states remained the places where their thinking about constitutions was most fully developed.

Chapter 3

The Crisis of the 1780s

It is difficult to explain the move for a new Constitution in the 1780s. In 1776 no one in his wildest dreams even imagined the kind of strong, far-removed, federal government that would be created a mere decade later. After all, the Americans had just thrown off a powerful distant government to preserve their liberty and scarcely seemed in any mood to think of creating another. If they had learned anything under the empire, it was that the closer the government was to the people, the safer and less tyrannical it was likely to be.

Besides, the best minds of the eighteenth century, including Montesquieu (whose *Spirit of the Laws* was in more libraries of the founders than any other work) had repeatedly told the world that republics necessarily had to be small in territory and homogeneous in population. Monarchies with their centralized authority and their hierarchical social structures and their standing armies could maintain themselves over large territories and diverse societies. But republics, which depended on the consent of the people, had none of the adhesives that held large monarchies together—force, kinship, patronage, and dependencies of various sorts. If republics became too large and composed of too many diverse interests, they were apt to fly apart.

Thus, people in a republic needed to rely on other sorts of social bonds—on their virtue, their affection for one another, and their willingness to sacrifice their selfish interests for the benefit of the whole. This is why republics were traditionally considered to be so vulnerable, so fragile, so likely to splinter into pieces.

For these reasons, the thirteen new independent republican states in 1776 had no intention of creating anything more than an alliance among themselves. The Articles of Confederation proposed by the Continental Congress in 1777 and ratified by all the states only in March 1781, six months before the battle of Yorktown, was about as far as most Americans at the outset were willing to go in creating a central government.[1]

The Confederation was scarcely a formidable central government. The Articles of Confederation was a treaty among thirteen sovereign states, an alliance that was not all that different from the present-day European Union. Each state had separate and equal representation in the Confederation Congress, and this treaty or alliance could not be altered without the agreement of every state. Although the Confederation may have been one of the strongest such unions in history, for its Congress was granted some substantial powers concerning war and diplomacy, the borrowing of money, and the requisitioning of troops, it ultimately lacked the crucial authority to tax and to regulate the commerce of the United States.[2] In fact, all final lawmaking authority remained with the individual states.

The Confederation had no real executive or judicial authority, and congressional resolutions were merely recommendations left to the states to enforce. To remove any doubts of the decentralized nature of this Confederation, Article 2 stated bluntly that "each State retains its sovereignty, freedom, and independence, and every power, jurisdiction, right, which is not by this confederation expressly delegated to the United States, in Congress, assembled."

The Articles of Confederation were not an early version of the later Constitution. The Confederation was an entirely different kind of union. It was not a government with a legislature, executive, and an independent judiciary similar to the governments of the individual states. It was intended to be and remained, as Article 3 declared, "a firm league of friendship," a treaty of alliance among thirteen states very jealous of their individual sovereignty.

Yet a brief ten years later, Americans ended up scrapping these Articles of Confederation and creating a totally new and powerful national government in its place. We are apt to assume that the transformation was inevitable, but we should not. It was a momentous change, and one not at all anticipated in 1776. The new government adopted in 1787–88 was not a stronger league of friendship with a few new powers added to the Congress. It was a radically new government altogether—one that utterly transformed the structure of central authority and greatly diminished the power of the several states. The Constitution of 1787 created a national republic in its own right, with a bicameral legislature, a single executive, and an independent supreme court—a government spanning half a continent that, unlike the Confederation, was designed to bypass the states and operate directly on individuals. It created in fact what a decade earlier had seemed theoretically impossible and virtually inconceivable.

Something awful had to have happened in the decade since independence for so many Americans to change their minds so dramatically about what kind of central government they would impose on themselves. What could have happened? What could have compelled Americans to put aside their earlier fears of far-removed political power and create such a strong national government? Today we take the Constitution and a powerful national government so much for granted that we can scarcely doubt its preordained creation. But perhaps we ought to wonder more why the Constitution needed to be created at all.

Nineteenth-century Americans tended to explain the Constitution in heroic terms. John Fiske, in a book published in 1888 for the centennial celebration of the Constitution, *The Critical Period of American History*, summed up this nineteenth-century thinking. "It is not to much to say," he wrote, "that the period of five years following the peace of 1783 was the most critical moment in all the history of the American people." And he made this extraordinary claim in the wake of the Civil War.[3]

Fiske pictured the 1780s as a time of chaos and anarchy, with the country's finances near ruin. The Confederation government was collapsing and the various state governments, beset by debtor and paper money advocates who were pressing creditor and commercial interests to the wall, were flying off in separate directions. It was a desperate situation retrieved only at the eleventh hour by the high-minded intervention of the founding fathers. These few great framers saved the country from disaster.

The problem with this dominant nineteenth-century interpretation is that there does not appear to have been any near collapse of the economy or any breakdown in society. There was no anarchy, no serious financial crisis, and apparently no real "critical period" after all.

Historical studies of the twentieth century tended to minimize the critical nature of the 1780s. Things seem not to have been as bad as John Fiske and the supporters of the Constitution, or the Federalists, as they called themselves, pictured them. This was the thrust of the work of the twentieth-century Progressive and neo-Progressive historians—beginning with Charles Beard at the start of the century and continuing into the final decades of the century with Merrill Jensen, and his students James Ferguson and Jackson Turner Main. "Clearly," wrote Ferguson, "it was not the era of public bankruptcy and currency depreciation that historians used to depict."[4] Both the Confederation and the state governments had done much to stabilize finances in the aftermath of the Revolution. The states had already begun assuming payment of the public debt, and the deficits were not really that serious. To be sure, there was economic dislocation and disruption, but there was no breakdown of the economy. There was a depression in 1784–85, but by 1786 the country was coming out of it, and many of the Federalists were aware of the returning prosperity. The commercial outlook was far from bleak. It's true that Americans were outside the mercantile protections of the British Empire, but they were freely trading with each other and were reaching out to ports throughout the world— to the West Indies and Spanish America, to the continent of Europe, to Alaska, to Russia, and even to China.

Contrary to Fiske's assessment, the 1780s were actually a time of great excitement and elevation of spirit. The country was bursting with energy and enterprise, and people were multiplying at a dizzying rate and were on the move in search of opportunities. They were spilling over the mountains into the newly acquired western territories with astonishing rapidity. Kentucky, which had virtually no white inhabitants at the time of independence, by 1780 already had 20,000 settlers.

Despite a slackening of immigration from abroad and the loss of tens of thousands of British loyalists, the population grew as never before or since. In fact, the 1780s experienced the fastest rate of demographic growth of any decade in all of American history. Men and women were marrying earlier and thus having more children—a measure of the high expectations and exuberance of the period.[5] "There is not upon the face of the earth a body of people more happy or rising into consequence with more rapid stride, than the Inhabitants of the United States of America," secretary of the Congress Charles Thomson told Thomas Jefferson in 1786. "Population is encreasing, new houses building, new settlements forming, and new manufactures establishing with a rapidity beyond conception."[6] Where did all the talk of crisis come from? "If we are undone," declared a bewildered South Carolinian, "we are the most splendidly ruined of any nation in the universe."[7]

There were economic problems, of course, "but," wrote historian Merrill Jensen, "there is no evidence of stagnation and decay in the 1780s." In fact, said Jensen, "the period was one of extraordinary growth."[8] It seems that the bulk of the society was seeking to fulfill the promise of the Revolution, and countless Americans were taking the pursuit of happiness seriously.

If all this is true, and the evidence is overwhelming that it is, then why did Americans create the Constitution? If the Confederation was not doing too bad a job of governing and commercial conditions in the 1780s were not actually desperate, why did something as extraordinary as the Constitution have to be created?

Answering these tough questions is no easy matter. The difficulty in explaining the creation of the Constitution led the twentieth-century Progressive and neo-Progressive historians to picture the move for a new national government as something of a conspiratorial fraud. The creation of the Constitution, they suggested, was the work of a tightly organized minority of continental-minded men who wished to reverse the democratic tendencies of the Revolution. The Constitution was a response out of all proportion to the social and economic reality of the time. The "critical period," wrote Charles Beard, was perhaps not so critical after all, "but a phantom of the imagination produced by some undoubted evils which could have been remedied without a political revolution." The conservative Federalists therefore had to exaggerate the anarchical conditions of the 1780s in order to justify the making of the Constitution. A sense of crisis, wrote Jackson Turner Main, had to be "conjured up" when "actually the country faced no such emergency."[9]

Charles Beard's *An Economic Interpretation of the Constitution* (1913) was the foundation of the Progressive argument. Beard pictured the Constitution as something foisted on the country by a minority of men with particular property interests that needed protection from rampaging democratic state legislatures. Although Beard's specific arguments and proofs have been eviscerated and were too crudely presented to be persuasive today, his book dominated the historical literature on the Constitution for much of the twentieth century, and it still casts a long shadow over writing about the Constitution. We can't get away from the Progressive and neo-Progressive argument that something other than the obvious weaknesses of the Confederation accounts for the Constitution.

But perhaps these weaknesses of the Confederation are by themselves sufficient to explain the move for the new Constitution. They certainly were formidable, and they became evident early, even before the Articles were formally ratified by all the states. By 1780 the war was dragging on longer than anyone expected, and the Continental Army was smoldering with resentment at the lack of pay and falling apart with desertions and even outbreaks of mutiny. By early 1781 the Confederation Congress could not even afford the cost of printing its own proceedings.

The Confederation's lack of taxing authority was becoming unbearable. The Congress borrowed huge amount of money from French and Dutch lenders and from its fellow Americans, but its ability to pay back its creditors seemed increasingly in doubt. When the Congress stopped paying interest on the public debt in the early

1780s, foreign and domestic creditors naturally wondered if the principal of the debt would ever be paid. The states were ignoring congressional resolutions and were refusing to supply their allotted contributions to the Congress. Since the Confederation Congress had no authority to regulate trade, the states were passing their own navigation acts, which complicated interstate commerce. Massachusetts, for example, was commercially treating Connecticut and Rhode Island as foreign nations.

By the mid-1780s a number of interest groups were working to strengthen the Confederation government. The former army officers, organized as the Order of the Cincinnati, were busy lobbying for a stronger Union. All those who held federal bonds and loan certificates were eager to grant the Congress the power to tax. Robert Morris, the wealthy Philadelphia merchant who had been appointed superintendent of finance in 1781, worked out a program of finance that anticipated Hamilton's a decade later. He sought to stabilize the economy, establish a bank, and get the commercial and financial groups more involved in the central government. Crucial to his plans for making the government's bonds more secure for investors was amending the Articles in order to grant the Congress the power to levy a 5 percent duty on imports. First Rhode Island and later New York refused to give the unanimous consent necessary for amending the Articles. Despite the frustration, however, by 1786 momentum was building to give some sort of taxing power to the Confederation Congress.

In a like manner, pressure was mounting to grant the Congress power to regulate international trade. Merchants with interstate connections, southern planters eager to open up foreign markets for their agricultural staples, and urban artisans anxious to get tariff protection from competitive European manufacturers—all wanted Congress to have the authority to pass navigation acts, levy tariffs, and retaliate against the British mercantile system. State and sectional jealousies blocked several attempts to grant the Congress a restricted power over commerce, but, as in the case of the taxing power, more and more interests were coming together in favor of some sort of commercial regulatory power being added to Congress.

At a meeting at Mount Vernon in 1785 Virginia and Maryland resolved a number of disputes concerning the navigation of Chesapeake Bay and the Potomac River. This conference suggested the advantages of thinking about reforming the Confederation outside the walls of Congress. This led to Virginia's invitation to the states to meet at Annapolis in 1786 to consider and recommend a federal plan for regulating commerce. In just this manner did the problems of commerce move the country toward reforming the Articles.[10]

At the same time a number of important leaders were becoming increasingly angry at the way various foreign powers were humiliating the new republic of the United States. Since American merchant ships lacked the protection of the British flag, many of them sailing in the Mediterranean were being seized by corsairs from the Muslim states of North Africa and their crews sold into slavery. The Congress had no money to pay for the necessary tribute and ransoms to these Barbary pirates.

In the late eighteenth-century world of hostile empires, it was difficult even for the new republican confederacy to maintain its territorial integrity. Britain refused to send a minister to the United States and was ignoring its treaty obligations to evacuate its military posts in the Northwest, claiming that the United States had not honored its own treaty commitments. The treaty of peace had specified that the Confederation would recommend to the states that confiscated loyalist property be restored and that neither side would make laws obstructing the recovery of prewar debts. When the states flouted these treaty obligations, the Congress could do nothing, and therefore British troops remained in Detroit, Niagara, Oswego, and other posts within American territory.

Britain was known to be plotting with the Indians and encouraging separatist movements in the Northwest and in the Vermont borderlands. Spain was doing the same in the Southwest and refused to recognize American claims to the territory between the Ohio River and Florida. In 1784, in an effort to influence American settlers moving into Kentucky and Tennessee, the Spanish government closed the Mississippi River to American trade. Many westerners were willing to deal with any government that could ensure access to the sea for their agricultural produce. They were "on a pivot," noted Washington in 1784. "The touch of a feather would turn them any way."[11]

Thus began the so-called Spanish conspiracy that eventually involved Spanish payments of money to several high officials of the American government, including Senator William Blount of Tennessee and James Wilkinson, the eventual commander in chief of the American army. The intrigues eventually came to a head in Aaron Burr's abortive plot in 1806–7 either to attack Mexico or to separate the western states from the Union.

In 1785–86 John Jay, a New Yorker and the secretary of foreign affairs, negotiated a treaty with the Spanish minister to the United States, Diego de Gardoqui. By the terms of this treaty Spain opened its empire to the trade of northern merchants in return for America's renunciation of its right to navigate the Mississippi for several decades. Fearing that the western settlers were being denied an outlet to the sea, the southern states, which assumed that they would be the source of most of the western settlers, prevented the necessary nine-state majority in the Congress from agreeing to the treaty. But the willingness of seven states to sacrifice western interests for the sake of northern merchants aroused long-existing sectional jealousies and threatened to shatter the Union. In an address to the Congress in August 1786 Jay defended his treaty on the grounds that it was the best the United States could get from Spain, at least until the Confederation "shall become more really and truly a nation than it is at present."[12]

All of these problems facing the Confederation in the 1780s were undoubtedly serious, but were they so serious that they couldn't have been remedied by amending the Articles of Confederation? Didn't the Constitution of 1787 go way beyond what the weaknesses of the Articles required and the various interest groups demanded?

Granting the Confederation Congress the authority to raise revenue, regulate trade, pay off its debts, and deal effectively in international affairs did not necessitate the total scrapping of the Articles and the formation of an extraordinarily powerful and distant national government the like of which was beyond anyone's imagination a decade earlier. Jefferson, who had been abroad since 1784, certainly thought that the Constitution of 1787 went much too far. It was not necessary, he told John Adams, to throw out the Articles of Confederation and replace it with an entirely new and stronger government. "Three or four new articles," he said, "might have been added to the good, old and venerable fabric" of the Confederation, and that would have been enough.[13]

By 1786 or so, most of the political nation agreed with that assessment. With the addition of a few powers, especially the power to tax, the Confederation could even have created a financial program similar to the one Hamilton created, funded its debts, passed navigation acts, and strengthened the country's position internationally.

But there was a much more serious problem than the obvious and generally acknowledged difficulties of credit, commerce, and foreign policy facing the country. That problem was democracy, excessive democracy, in the states, and it was a problem the Confederation, however amended, however strengthened, could not handle. That problem of excessive democracy in the states created a sense of a genuine crisis among many leaders that required the scrapping of the Articles and the formation of the new Constitution.

The American Revolution turned out to be much more revolutionary and radical than many of the leaders expected. It released the aspirations and interests of tens upon tens of thousands of middling people—commercial farmers, petty merchants, small-time traders, and artisans of various sorts—all eager to buy and sell and get rich. Of course, they went into debt and urged the printing of paper money. But debt was not necessarily a sign of poverty; indeed, it was often a sign of ambitious aspirations. And paper money was not simply designed to relieve debt. It was capital, and it was necessary for buying more land or livestock or setting up a shop or fulfilling other dreams.

These aspiring and commercially minded middling people began electing to the greatly enlarged state legislatures ordinary middling men like themselves in increasing numbers, men like William Findley, a Scotch-Irish immigrant and ex-weaver from western Pennsylvania, and Abraham Yates, a former shoemaker from Albany. These middling legislators were shrewd and smart, but they had not gone to college and were not considered gentlemen by the standards of the time. And they were using the electoral process and the Revolutionary emphasis on equality to vault into power in the state legislatures and promote the economic interests of their middling constituents. The state legislatures, complained the aristocratic Robert R. Livingston of New York, have become full of men "unimproved by education and unreformed by honor."[14] This was the excessive democracy that lay behind the creation of the Constitution.

No one in the 1780s saw what was happening more clearly than James Madison. He became the most important figure in the creation of the new federal government. Early in 1787 he put his ideas together in a working paper that he called "Vices of the Political System of the United States." In this paper, which was the most important document dealing with American constitutionalism between the Articles of Confederation and the Constitution, Madison spent very little time on the weaknesses of the Confederation. Instead, he concentrated on the deficiencies of the state governments, on what he called the "multiplicity," "mutability," and "injustice" of the laws the states were passing. Especially alarming in his eyes were the paper money emissions, stay laws, and other debtor relief legislation that hurt the minority of creditors and violated individual property rights.[15]

Madison did not come to these ideas from all the books his friend Jefferson was sending him from Europe. He learned about the vices of state politics firsthand—from being a member of the Virginia state assembly from 1784 to 1787. This was a frustrating and disillusioning experience for Madison, for it revealed to him what democracy had come to mean in America.

Although Madison had some notable legislative achievements, namely his shepherding into enactment Jefferson's famous bill for religious freedom, he was continually exasperated by what Jefferson later called (no doubt following Madison's own account) "the endless quibbles, chicaneries, perversions, vexations, and delays of lawyers and demi-lawyers" in the assembly.[16] The legislators seemed so narrow-minded, so parochial, and so illiberal; indeed, these were the code words that Madison always used to describe these deplorable middling legislators. Such men rarely had any concern for public honor or honesty and always seemed to have "a particular interest to serve" regardless of the needs of the whole state or the nation. They made a travesty of the legislative process and were reluctant to do anything that might appear unpopular with their constituents. They postponed taxes, subverted debts owed to the subjects of Great Britain, and passed, defeated, and repassed bills in the most haphazard manner.[17]

Most of his and Jefferson's plans for legal reform were undermined by the localism of these narrow-minded legislators. "Important bills prepared at leisure by skillful hands," he complained, were mauled and torn apart by "crudeness and tedious discussion." Madison repeatedly found himself having to beat back the "itch for paper money" and other measures "of a popular cast." Too often, he admitted, he could plan only on "moderating the fury," not defeating it.[18]

This was not what republican lawmaking was supposed to be. Madison repeatedly had to make concessions to the "prevailing sentiments," whether or not such sentiments promoted the good of the state of the nation. He had to agree to bad laws for fear of getting worse ones, and he had to give up good bills "rather than pay such a price" as these small-minded, illiberal legislators wanted.[19] Today legislators are used to this sort of political horse-trading. But Madison was not yet ready for the logrolling and the pork-barreling that would eventually become the staples of American legislative politics.

By 1786 he knew that appealing to the people had none of the beneficial effects good republicans had expected. A bill having to do with court reform, for example, was "to be printed for the consideration of the public." But "instead of calling forth the sanction of the wise & judicious," this action, Madison feared, would only "be a signal to interested men to redouble their efforts to get into the Legislature."[20] Democracy was no solution to the problem; democracy was the problem.

Madison realized that these state legislators were expressing only the narrow interests and parochial outlooks of their constituents. Too many American people could not see beyond their own pocketbooks or their own neighborhoods. "Individuals of extended views, and of national pride," said Madison, might be able to bring public proceedings to an enlightened cosmopolitan standard, but their example would never be followed by "the multitude." "Is it to be imagined," he asked, "that an ordinary citizen or even an assembly man of R. Island in estimating the policy of paper money, ever considered or cared in what light the measure would be viewed in France or Holland; or even in Massachusetts or Connecticut? It was a sufficient temptation to both that it was for their interest."[21]

But Rhode Island was not the only state passing paper money emissions. Printing paper money and making it legal tender were the state laws that Madison considered most unjust to minorities, and nearly every state was abusing the practice. Since many members of the wealthy elites often acted as bankers in their communities and lived off the interest from their money out on loan, they found the inflation caused by the excessive printing of paper money devastating. "A depreciating Currency," warned John Adams at the outset in 1777, "will ruin us." Washington, who was both a planter and a banker, became furious with the way his debtors had used the deprecation of paper money to scam him while he was away fighting the British. These scoundrels, he complained, had "taken advantage of my absence and the tender laws, to discharge their debts with a shilling or a six pence to the pound." At the same time, he had "to pay in specie at the real value" to those British merchants in London to whom he owed money. Rather than enter into litigation, however, "unless there is every reason to expect a decision in my favor," Washington told his agent to agree to accept paper money in place of specie for his rents and the debts owed him, "however unjustly and rascally it has been imposed." No wonder then, said Robert Morris, that wealthy men, at least those who had survived the Revolution, had more or less ceased playing the role of bankers and had stopped taking up bonds and mortgages; they were naturally "deterred from lending money again by the dread of paper money and tender laws."[22]

This shows that Madison's experience with the popular politics of the state legislatures was not unusual; otherwise, he could never have gained support for what he wanted to do. Others, too, were appalled by the chaos of middle-class lawmaking in the states. Laws, as the Vermont Council of Censors declared in 1786, were "altered—realtered—made better—made worse, and kept in such a fluctuating position that persons in civil commissions scarce know what is law."[23] Indeed, said Madison in his "Vices" essay, more laws had been passed in the decade since independence than in the entire colonial period. All this was the result of the rapid turnover of membership in the state legislatures, which often approached 60 percent annually, and the incessant scrambling among different shifting interests in societies eager to use state lawmaking to promote their causes.

By the mid-1780s groups of "gentlemen" up and down the continents were horrified by the "private views and selfish principles" of the kind of men who had come to dominate the state legislatures. "Although there are no nobles in America," observed the French minister Louis Otto, "there is a class of men denominated 'gentlemen,' who by reason of their wealth, their talents, their education, or the offices they hold, aspire to a preeminence which the people refuse to grant them."[24] Obviously, this is an exaggeration since the people, especially in the South, were more than willing to elect gentlemen to offices. But Otto had a point, as increasing numbers of middling men were challenging the gentlemen for leadership and unsettling the older social hierarchies.

These uneducated middling sorts, the gentry complained, were "men of narrow souls and no natural interest in the society." They were self-serving, ignorant, illiberal men who were bringing discredit upon popular government. They were promoting special interests at the expense of the whole, pandering "to the vulgar and sordid notions of the populace," and acting as judges in their own causes.[25]

Everywhere localism was preventing legislators from looking after the general good of the states or the nation. The representatives in all the state assemblies, observed Ezra Stiles, president of Yale College, were concerned with only the special interests of their electors. Whenever a bill was read in the legislature, he noted, "every one instantly thinks how it will affect his constituents."[26] This sort of extreme democracy was not what many American leaders had expected from the Revolution.

By the mid-1780s many American gentry were convinced that majority factions within the state legislatures had become the greatest source of tyranny in America. Although some Tory loyalists had warned at the outset that popularly elected institutions might become tyrannical, the patriots had dismissed such warnings out of hand. The people, who loved liberty, could never tyrannize themselves. The idea, said John Adams in 1775, was illogical; "a democratic despotism was a contradiction in terms."[27]

But the experience since independence had changed many minds, including Adams's. The legislatures, however representative, however frequently elected, were quite capable of tyranny. It did not matter how many representatives there were. "173 despots," said Jefferson, "would surely be as oppressive as one."[28] But, unlike his friend Madison, Jefferson always thought the abusive state assemblymen had drifted away from the people, whose virtue he never doubted. By contrast, Madison realized that the rampaging state legislatures were often only too representative of the people.

These legislative abuses, these "excesses of democracy," were not like the deficiencies of the Confederation; they were not easily remedied, for Madison and his colleagues knew only too well that there were no amendments to the Articles that could lessen these wild and unjust expressions of democracy. These legislature abuses were inherent in what the Revolution and republicanism were about. They "brought into question," said Madison, with about as much honesty and candor as one could expect, "the fundamental principle of republican Government, that the majority who rule in such Governments are the safest Guardians both of public Good and private rights."[29]

Initially, leaders had responded to these problems of state legislative tyranny by proposing changes in the state governments and state constitutions. Reformers sought to take back some of the powers that the revolutionary constitutions of 1776 had granted the state legislatures, particularly the lower houses of representatives. They tried to strengthen the senators, governors, and judiciaries, and to reduce the democratic character of the state governments. These reformers were most successful with the Massachusetts constitution of 1780, drawn up by a committee led by John Adams. This belatedly drafted constitution benefited from the woeful experiences of the earlier revolutionary constitutions and sought to redress the mistakes they had made. Unlike the earlier constitutions, the Massachusetts constitution gave the governor an extraordinary degree of power, including the power of appointment and a limited veto over all legislation. Such a conservative constitution formed a model for others of what state reformers should aim for.

Thus, when a rebellion of nearly two thousand debtor farmers led by a former militia captain Daniel Shays broke out in Massachusetts in late 1786, many leaders were surprised. The Massachusetts constitution had seemed so stable and so capable of handling things. But more alarming than the rebellion itself was the fact that Shays's sympathizers were seeking election to the Massachusetts legislature and enacting into law debtor relief legislation that they were unable to get by forcibly closing the courts. With "a total change of men" in the legislature said Noah Webster, a Yale graduate and the later creator of an American dictionary of the English language, "there will be, therefore, no further insurrection, because the Legislature will represent the sentiments of the people." This expression of democracy led some Americans to complain that "sedition itself will sometimes make law."[30]

Shays's Rebellion convinced many that relief from the democratic excesses could not be found at the state level. If the model conservative constitution of Massachusetts couldn't contain the popular pressures, then no state could. But well before Shays's Rebellion, Madison and other leaders had already decided that reform of the state constitutions would not be enough to solve the problems of popular politics within the states. "In vain," said wealthy Massachusetts merchant Stephen Higginson, "must be all our exertions to brace up our own Government without we have a better federal system than at present."[31] Something had to be done at the national level.

Because nearly everyone in the political nation was prepared by 1786 or so to grant the Confederation Congress taxing and trade regulatory powers, Madison and his colleagues saw an opening and they took it. The convention in Annapolis in September 1786 called to decide trade matters for the Congress was attended by only five states, but its participants used the opportunity to ask the Congress to authorize a meeting in Philadelphia in May 1787 of all the states "to devise such further provisions as should appear to them necessary to render the constitution of federal government adequate to the exigencies of the union."[32]

Most people assumed that this May meeting in Philadelphia would finally add those amendments to the Articles that nearly everyone desired. In effect, Madison and his colleagues hijacked this reform effort and used it as a cover for an entirely different plan of reform.

Many of the delegates to the Philadelphia Convention in May 1787 were no longer interested in simply modifying the Articles of Confederation. They wanted to weaken, if not destroy, the states and the democratic excesses they had generated. "The vile State governments are the source of pollution, which will contaminate the American name for ages. . . . Smite them," Henry Knox urged Rufus King, who was attending the Convention, "Smite them in the name of God and the people."[33]

The stakes involved in this Convention could not have been higher. The meeting in Philadelphia, said Madison, was meant to "decide forever the fate of republican government."[34]

Chapter 4

The Federal Constitution

James Madison and his nationalist-minded colleagues knew that they would never be able to get any substantial changes in the federal government through the Confederation Congress. People were proposing amendments to the Articles in the Congress, but they were going nowhere. Sectional tensions stemming from the aborted Spanish treaty made agreement among the congressional delegates impossible. But Madison and his fellow nationalists had already decided to bypass the Congress and use the upcoming convention in Philadelphia to bring about the necessary changes in the federal government. In an attempt to salvage some of its dignity, the Congress in February 1787 belatedly authorized the Convention due to meet in May "for the sole and express purpose of revising the Articles of Confederation." Little did many members of the Congress know what Madison and his Virginia delegation to the Convention had in mind.[1]

Although the Congress may have been uneasy about what was going on, the situation seemed so dire that most Americans, some reluctantly, agreed that this meeting in Philadelphia ought to occur. Most knew that the Articles of Confederation were deficient, and that some amendments had to be added to the league of states. The Articles were practically defunct anyhow. Not a single state was complying with the requisitions, and no money was being paid into the public treasury. Even the members of the Congress, noted Madison, "agreed that the federal government in its existing shape was inefficient and could not last long."[2]

William Findley, a member of the Pennsylvania assembly from the Pittsburgh area and one of the narrow-minded and illiberal promoters of paper money whom Madison deplored, was asked by his state legislature whether he would like to be one of Pennsylvania's delegates to the Convention in Philadelphia. When told that the state would not pay for his living expenses while he was in Philadelphia, Findley declined the invitation. He didn't have the kind of wealth that the rich merchant Robert Morris did to support weeks of living at an inn. Consequently, Pennsylvania's delegation of seven members, including Robert Morris, all came from the city of Philadelphia, and one of them, Gouverneur Morris (no relation), was a New Yorker and not even a citizen of Pennsylvania.

Findley, who later became a fiery opponent of the Constitution, had no idea that the Convention was going to do what it did—scrap the Articles, not amend them, and create an entirely new and powerful government in their place—all in violation of what the Confederation Congress had authorized. John Tyler of Virginia had expected the Convention simply to vote to add to the Articles a necessary power to regulate commerce. "But," he said when he saw the results, "it had never entered my head we should quit liberty and throw ourselves in the hands of an energetic government." Others agreed that they had gotten more than they had expected. Had the American people known beforehand what the Convention was up to, "probably no state," said "The Federal Farmer" (likely Melancton Smith, a New Yorker), the most literate and powerful writer opposing the Constitution, said that had the American people known beforehand what the Convention was up to, "probably no state would have appointed members to the convention.... Probably not one man in ten thousand in the United States ... had an idea that the old ship was to be destroyed."[3]

Startling as it was, the Constitution that emerged from the Convention in September 1787 was not the half of it. If those who were surprised at the extraordinary nature of the national government created by the Constitution had known what had actually gone on in the Convention, they would have been even more shocked. The national government that came out of the Convention was much less powerful than many of the delegates had wanted. The Constitution was a compromise; indeed, in the eyes of some of the leading delegates, including James Madison, it was a failure, inadequate to the crisis facing the nation and probably doomed to collapse. Three and a half months of deliberation and debates at Philadelphia had forced concessions and changes and had created something that no one at the outset had anticipated.

Fifty-five delegates representing twelve states attended the Convention in Philadelphia in the summer of 1787, from May 13 to September 18. Although many of the delegates were young men—their average age was forty-two—most were well educated and experienced members of America's political elite.[4] Thirty-nine had served in the Continental and Confederation Congress at one time or another, eight had worked in the state constitutional conventions, seven had been state governors, and thirty-four were lawyers. One-third were veterans of the Continental Army, that great dissolver of state loyalties, as Washington described it. Nearly all were gentlemen, "natural aristocrats," who took their political superiority for granted as the inevitable consequence of their social and economic position.

The delegates naturally chose Washington as president of the Convention. Some of the leading figures of the Revolution were not present. Samuel Adams was ill. Thomas Jefferson and John Adams were serving as ministers abroad, and Richard Henry Lee and Patrick Henry, although selected by the Virginia legislature as delegates, refused to attend. "I smelt a Rat," Henry allegedly said.[5] The most influential delegations were those of Pennsylvania and Virginia, which included Gouverneur Morris and James Wilson of Pennsylvania, and Edmund Randolph, George Mason, and James Madison of Virginia.

It was a loaded convention. Nearly everyone present was a nationalist and suspicious of state-based democracy. When two of the delegates from New York, Robert Yates and John Lansing, who were not nationalists, came to appreciate the direction the Convention was taking, they bailed out and left the New York delegation without a quorum and unable to record a vote. This is why the Convention's letter of September 17, 1787, sending the final Constitution on to the Congress, lists the states present and voting as "New Hampshire, Massachusetts, Connecticut, Mr. Hamilton from New York, New Jersey," and so on with the listing of the rest of the states.

The Convention was supposed to begin on May 13 but not until May 25 was a quorum of states present and not until May 29 did the Convention get down to serious business. The delegates immediately took extraordinary steps to keep their proceedings secret: no copies of anything in their journal were to be communicated to the outside society, and sentries were even posted to keep out intruders. This sensitivity to the public out-of-doors was new; the state constitutional conventions a decade earlier had never made such decisions concerning secrecy. But since 1776 many members of the elite had discovered that there were emerging popular politicians everywhere eager to pounce on anything that might discredit the established leaders. If the Convention's deliberations were likely to be picked up by "imprudent printers" and conveyed to "the too credulous and unthinking mobility," then the delegates' freedom to discuss issue openly and candidly would be seriously inhibited. Madison later reportedly declared that "no Constitution would ever have been adopted by the convention if the debates had been public."[6]

The Virginia delegation took the lead and presented the Convention with its first working proposal. This Virginia plan was largely the effort of the thirty-six-year-old Madison, who more than any other person deserves the title "Father of the Constitution." Short, shy, and soft-spoken, he had graduated from the College of New Jersey (Princeton), one of the few southerners to attend that Presbyterian college. He had read some law, but had not trained for any particular profession. He possessed a sharp and questioning mind, and, supported by his father's slaveholding plantation, he had devoted his life to public service. He understood clearly the historical significance of the meeting of the Convention. It is because he decided to make a detailed private record of the Convention debates that we know so much of what was said that summer in Philadelphia.

The Virginia plan, presented by Governor Edmund Randolph, was breathtaking. When Randolph moved at the outset that the Convention commit itself to the proposition "that a national government ought to be established consisting of a supreme legislature, judiciary, and executive," many of the delegates were stunned.[7] They realized that this Virginia plan involved much more than simply amending the Articles. No mere tinkering with the Articles, no mere expedients, would suffice any longer. Indeed, Madison's ideas of reform embodied in the Virginia plan, as he put it, "strike so deeply at the old Confederation, and lead to such a systematic change, that they scarcely admit of the expedient." Madison wanted to create a general government that would exercise direct power over individuals and be organized as most of the state governments were organized, with a single executive, a bicameral legislature, and a separate judiciary. He was willing to keep the states in the system, he said, but certainly they could not retain any of their "individual independence." His idea of a "middle ground" was "a due supremacy of the national authority," while leaving "in force the local authorities in so far as they can be useful."[8] This was a far cry from the federalism of the Articles of Confederation.

According to the Virginia plan, representation in both houses of the legislature would be in proportion to population or to the contribution of taxes or to both. The lower house would be elected directly by the people; the upper house would be elected by the lower house from lists of persons nominated by the states. The national executive, the number of which was not specified, would be chosen by the national legislature for a single term of years. The national judiciary, made up of both superior and inferior courts, was to be chosen by the national legislature. The Virginia plan also provided for a council of revision composed of the executive and a number of the national judiciary with a limited veto power over acts of both the national legislature and the state legislatures.

Since the evils of the 1780s flowed from "the turbulence and follies of democracy" within the states, the new government, said Randolph, was to be "a strong, *consolidated* union, in which the idea of the states should be nearly annihilated."[9] Thus the Virginia plan gave the national legislature the authority to legislate "in all cases to which the states are incompetent" and the power to veto or "to negative all laws passed by the several States, contravening in the opinion of the National Legislature, the articles of Union." This was not quite what Madison had in mind a month or two earlier. He originally had wanted his congressional negative on state legislation to apply "in all cases whatsoever"—a phase so frightening, echoing as it did Parliament's Declaratory Act of 1766, that his colleagues had the good sense to drop it in the final Virginia plan.[10]

This power to negative all state laws contravening the Union was in addition to the veto power over state laws given to the proposed council of revision. This double veto of state legislation was a measure of Madison's deep revulsion with what the states had been doing in the 1780s. He believed the national legislature's proposed veto authority over state legislation "to be absolutely necessary, and to be the least possible encroachment on the State jurisdictions." It would enable the national government to play the same role the English Crown had been supposed to play in the British Empire—that of a "disinterested & dispassionate umpire" over clashing interests.[11] By a vote of six states to one, the Convention agreed at the outset to make the Virginia plan the basis for its opening deliberations.

The delegates found it difficult to agree on any one thing, because agreement on one part of the government would later be unsettled by changes made in another part. Some, for example, were reluctant to agree on an executive of one person or several persons until they knew the extent of authority the executive would be granted. Despite fear of creating an elective monarchy, the Convention eventually agreed on a single executive with power to execute the laws.

But agreement on these sorts of matters could not hide the basic chasm that was opening up as the delegates became aware of the implications of the Virginia plan. The plan seemed to some delegates to be too consolidating, too nationalistic. It tended to swallow up the states and undermine their integrity. While nearly all the delegates at Philadelphia were eager to create a stronger central government, some of them soon came to realize that the Virginia plan went further than they wanted to go.

The issue was first raised on June 9 by William Paterson of New Jersey. He was bothered by the Virginia plan's proposal that both houses of the national legislature be proportionally representative. This, said Paterson, would destroy the sovereignty of each of the states and place majority power in the hands of the representatives of the large populous states. New Jersey, he warned, would never agree to confederate on these terms. James Wilson of Pennsylvania retorted hotly that the people of his state would never confederate if each state were to have equal representation in the national legislature. Two days later, on June 11, the Convention reaffirmed the principle of proportional representation embodied in the Virginia plan, but the vote for proportional representation for the upper house, which would become the Senate, was close, six states to five.

This vote galvanized the opposition. On June 15 Paterson proposed nine resolutions, which became the New Jersey plan. These were essentially nine amendments to the Articles of Confederation, maintaining the basic structure of the old Confederation with the equal representation of each state in the Congress but granting to the Congress all the powers of taxation and regulating commerce that most leaders in the 1780s had wanted. New Jersey was supported by the delegates from Connecticut, New York, and Delaware. Paterson and most of the other supporters of the New Jersey plan were not opposed to a strong national government, but, as John Dickinson warned Madison, they thought the Virginia plan was "pushing things too far." As much as they wanted "a good National Government," they would never allow the states to be totally swallowed up.[12] With two such different proposals before it, the Convention was at a crisis.

On June 18, in the midst of this debate over the Virginia and New Jersey plans, Alexander Hamilton of New York suddenly rose and made his own personal proposal for a government in a four- to five-hour-long speech. His proposed government was consolidated to the extreme, virtually abolishing the states as independent entities. He wanted an executive and senate elected for life, with the executive to have absolute veto power over all legislation. The states would remain as administrative units with their governors appointed by the national government. He accompanied his plan with praise of the English constitution and criticism of the Virginia plan.

Although Hamilton's speech has puzzled historians, the timing of it suggests that he probably saw his extreme proposal as a means of making the Virginia plan seem more moderate, as a middle-of-the-road compromise between his plan and the New Jersey plan. He certainly went out of his way to lump the Virginia plan together with the New Jersey plan as inadequate to deal with "the violence and turbulence of democratic government." "The Virginia plan," he said, was "pork still, with little change of sauce."[13]

Maybe it worked, for on June 19 the Convention voted for the Virginia plan against the New Jersey plan, seven states to three, with one divided. This was a crucial vote. It meant that the basic principle of the Articles—equal state sovereignty—was rejected. The new national government was not to be a league of states but a government in its own right. But the struggle over the precise role of the states in this national government was not over. It occupied the Convention in heated debates for a month longer. As Luther Martin of Maryland later recalled, throughout that time the delegates "were on the verge of dissolution, scarce held together by the strength of a hair."[14]

Historians have often pictured the debate over representation of states in the national government as one between the small states and the large states. This is misleading. Madison and Wilson, it is true, were delegates from the large, populous states of Virginia and Pennsylvania, but their opposition to equal representation of the states in either branch of the national legislature was not based simply on a parochial concern with the interests of their respective states. Madison and Wilson were more cosmopolitan and far-sighted than that. To them the issue of the debate was whether or not any semblance of the old Confederation would remain in the new Constitution. Those nationalists who believed that all the ills of the 1780s flowed from the vicious behavior of the state legislatures were worried that any equal representation of the states in the new national legislature would in effect perpetuate the state sovereignty that had vitiated the Confederation. If the Senate should contain equal representation of each state, it would be only a matter of time before the states would overawe and dominate the national government. It was for this reason that nationalists like Madison and Wilson so vehemently opposed equal representation of the states in the Senate; they wanted proportional representation in both houses.

After a month of deliberation, the crucial vote was taken on July 16. The result was the so-called Connecticut compromise, by which each state secured two senators in the upper house, carried by five states to four, with one divided.[15] Madison was beside himself with anger and anguish. He did not regard the states' equal representation in the Senate as a "compromise." For him and the other nationalists it was a defeat, pure and simple. The "Connecticut compromise" allowed the states to get back into the national government after the Virginia plan had banished them. Indeed, the Virginia plan, with its broad grant of powers to the national legislature and its veto over all state laws, depended on keeping the states as states entirely out of the national government. With this "compromise" the sovereignty of the states was once more in play.

The Virginia delegation was in despair, and Randolph proposed that the Convention adjourn temporarily in order to give both sides time to "consider the steps proper to be taken in the present solemn crisis of the business."[16] The next morning, July 17, the Virginia delegates and some other nationalists caucused to decide whether they should pull out of the Convention, but they were divided, and nothing was done. As Madison observed, this was tantamount to accepting the equality of the states in the Senate.

This nationalist defeat had implications for the whole initial Virginia plan. The "Connecticut compromise" forced a series of changes and adjustments: the powers of the legislature had to be clarified, the nature and election of the executive had to be worked out, and the authority of the judiciary needed to be modified.

In place of the broad and indefinite legislative authority granted by the Virginia plan, the Congress was granted a list of specific powers, which became Article I, Section 8, of the final Constitution. And the authority of the legislature to veto all state laws was abandoned, much to Madison's great chagrin. In its stead, the Convention presented a series of prohibitions on the states, which became Article I, Section 10, of the Constitution. The states were forbidden to levy customs duties on imports or exports, to enter into treaties, to coin money, to emit paper money, and to pass bills of attainder, ex post facto laws, or laws impairing contracts.

These prohibitions were serious. Not only were they directed at the principal legislative vices of the 1780s, but they in effect promised to render the states nearly economically incompetent. In that premodern world customs duties were the most common and efficient form of taxation. With the Constitution the states would lose not only this major source of revenue but also the capacity to print paper money and make it legal tender—something that the colonies and later the states had frequently used during the eighteenth century. At a stroke, the Constitution forbade what the British government in its various currency acts had earlier tried to do.

Madison took the loss of the national legislature's negative over all state laws very hard. Without the negative, he told Jefferson in the fall of 1787, the Constitution would not answer its purposes: it would neither solve the national problems of the Confederation "nor prevent the local mischiefs which everywhere excite disgust against the state governments."[17] Madison had little confidence in the suggestion made by some that the national judiciary might be able to keep the state legislatures within bounds.

Several of the delegates were, indeed, coming to count on the judiciary increasingly to curb democratic excesses. Early on, the Convention had rejected Madison's plan for a joint executive-judicial council of revision with a limited veto power over both national and state legislation. Most of the delegates thought the judges by themselves could set aside unconstitutional laws and ought not to be mixed up in the passing of these laws. Despite the persistent efforts of Madison and other nationalists to revive the council of revision, the decision to have the judiciary stand alone held.

Far more attention was paid to the executive than to the judiciary. Originally the executive, like the state governors, was to have only restricted powers. Though the president (a shrewdly chosen title) was granted limited veto power over acts of Congress and was made commander in chief of the armed forces, the Committee of Detail initially gave to the Senate sole authority to appoint ambassadors and justices of the Supreme Court and to make foreign treaties. But once Madison and the other nationalists realized the implications of state influence in the Senate following the compromise of July 16, they decided to place these powers in the hands of the president, with the Senate's authority reduced to advising and consenting only.

The compromise of July 16 also affected the mode of electing the president. If he were elected by the whole Congress, including a Senate in which the states would have equal representation, it was feared that he might become a captive of state interests. To avoid this and to keep the executive independent of the legislature, some suggested that his election by Congress be for a single seven-year term without the possibility of re-election. But that seemed to be too long a term. Others, like James Wilson, wanted the president elected directly by the people. (Wilson, in his arrogance, had no objection to the people en masse; it was middling individuals he found contemptible.) But the delegates did not anticipate political parties with tickets and party-selected candidates. They also did not foresee the important role that newspapers would come to play in party politics. After Washington's election, how would the people in such a huge nation know who were the men best qualified to be president? In a direct election by the people, how would someone in Georgia, for example, know who in New Hampshire or Connecticut was a suitable person to be president?

Finally, after much discussion and many votes, the Convention decided to create an alternative Congress composed of notables who would know who was competent to be president; it would have one function: to elect the president every four years. This electoral college seemed to solve all the problems. It guaranteed the president's independence from Congress without limiting the terms of office. And yet, as an exact replica of Congress, it had all the advantages of the July 16 compromise on representation between the nationally minded delegates and the small-state delegates.

Many expected the electoral college to work as a nominating body in which no one normally would get a majority of electoral votes; therefore, most elections would take place in the House of Representatives among the top five candidates, with each state's congressional delegation voting as a unit. The electoral college was an ingenious solution to delicate and controversial political problems, and the fact that it has rarely worked the way it was intended does not change its ingeniousness.[18]

In the end Madison and other nationalists were very pessimistic about the Constitution. Washington is supposed to have said that the new government wouldn't last twenty years. As a remedy for the democratic ills of the 1780s, it fell short of the mark. Still, it was better than the Articles of Confederation, and Madison and Hamilton began working for its ratification by the states.

Together with John Jay, they wrote under the pseudonym "Publius" eighty-five papers, published initially in newspapers between October 1787 and the summer of 1788 and later collected in book form as *The Federalist*. The essays were designed principally to convince New Yorkers to ratify the new document. Precisely because the issue of the Constitution's republican character seemed so much in doubt, the authors spent a considerable amount of time describing just how republican the new government was. In the Constitution, wrote Madison in *Federalist* No. 10, "we behold a republican remedy for the diseases most incident to republicanism."[19]

But how was it a remedy? Why was the new federal government better able to deal with the popular vices of the system than the states? Since both were republics with elected legislatures, why should the Congress of the national government be trusted and the legislatures of the states not trusted? In what ways was Congress different from the state governments?

Madison, for one, saw the relevance of these questions. "It may be asked," he told Jefferson a month after the Convention adjourned, "how private rights will be more secure under the Guardianship of the General Government than under the State governments, since they are both founded on the republican principle which refers the ultimate decision to the will of the majority."[20] What, in other words, would keep the new national government from succumbing to the same popular pressures, the same vices, that had afflicted the state governments? How could the new federal government avoid the same problems of excessive democracy that had plagued the states?

The answers that the supporters of the Constitution—or the Federalists, as they shrewdly called themselves—gave to these questions reveals their elitist social perspective. They believed that they could trust the national government more than the state governments because they expected different sorts of men to sit in the national government from those who sat in the legislatures of the state governments. They believed that most of the problems of majoritarian factionalism and popular politics in the state legislatures came from the narrow-minded middling kinds of people getting elected to these legislatures. The Federalists thought that too many of the state legislators were obscure and ordinary men with "factious tempers" and "localist prejudices," middling men like William Findley, who were bypassing traditional gentry leadership and using popular demagogic skills to vault into power in the state legislatures.[21]

The Federalists hoped that the elevated nature of the new national government would keep such illiberal and narrow-minded men out of government and allow more educated, more cosmopolitan, and more enlightened sorts of men to hold office. Madison called the process by which this would take place one of "filtration." By enlarging the electorate and decreasing the number of representatives, the new federal structure would ensure that better sorts of men would be elected, "men," wrote Madison in *The Federalist*, "who possess the most attractive merit and the most diffusive and established character."[22]

The five congressmen from North Carolina in the new government, for example, were apt to be more respectable and more enlightened, more apt to be college graduates, more apt to be gentlemen than the 232 who sat in the North Carolina legislature. The first House of Representatives in the Congress comprised only sixty-five members, a group smaller than most of the state legislatures, and these fewer members were more likely to be better educated and more cosmopolitan than the hundreds who sat in the various state legislatures. Or so the Federalists hoped.

No one tried to work out the intellectual and theoretical implications of the new government more thoroughly or more consistently than Madison. Madison turned the traditional assumptions about republicanism on their head. Instead of agreeing with Montesquieu that a republic has to be small in size and homogeneous in interests, Madison borrowed an insight from Scottish philosopher David Hume and argued that a republic was most suited to a large territory with a heterogeneity of interests. "What remedy can be found in a republican Government, where the majority must ultimately decide," Madison argued, "but that of giving such an extent to its sphere, that no one common interest or passion will be likely to unite a majority of the whole number in an unjust pursuit."[23] The large extent and the elevated nature of the new national government was the best way of dealing with democratic passions and interests.

But Madison did not expect the new national government to have no common interest or no public good to promote. "I mean not by these remarks," he cautioned Jefferson, "to insinuate that an esprit de corps will not exist in the national Government."[24] Madison was not an originator of what is now called an "interest group" or a "pluralist" conception of politics. Despite his hardheaded appreciation of the prevalence of interests in politics, he did not believe that public policy or the common good would emerge naturally from the give-and-take of hosts of competing interests. Instead, he hoped that these clashing interests and factions in an enlarged national republic would neutralize themselves and thereby allow liberally educated, rational men "whose enlightened views and virtuous sentiments," said Madison, "render them superior to local prejudices and to schemes of injustice," to promote the public good in an disinterested manner.[25]

It worked that way in religion, he said. The multiplicity of religious denominations in America prevented any one of them from dominating and thus permitted the enlightened reason of secular-minded men like Madison and Jefferson to shape public policy and church-state relations. He had gained this insight when he success-fully shepherded Jefferson's bill for religious freedom through the Virginia legislature. Although Jefferson thought that his bill became law because enlightened reason had spread through Virginia's so-ciety, Madison knew better. It was the competition among the various denominations in the state—Presbyterians, Baptists, Methodists, Quakers—that enabled Jefferson's bill to pass. Each of the denominations feared that one of the others might replace the Anglicans as the established church. Rather than let that happen, they all agreed to neutralize the state's role in religion. Nothing like that had ever occurred before in Western history. This was not tol-eration, which was already acceptable in Britain and parts of Europe and implied an establishment that tolerated dissenters; this was true religious liberty, with the state having no role whatsoever in reli-gious life. Madison took the lesson to heart and applied it to the new federal government in *Federalist* No. 51.

To the amazement of many, this separation of church and state did not lead to any loss of religious fervor; indeed, religious enthu-siasm increased in the decades following the Revolution, as the hordes of middling people moving upward in the society brought their religiosity with them.

The opponents of the Constitution, the Anti-Federalists as they were labeled, saw very clearly what Madison and the Federalists were up to. But instead of seeing enlightened patriots simply making a constitution to promote the national interest, they saw groups of interested gentry trying to foist an "aristocracy" onto republican America. They reacted by attacking the Constitution for being an aristocratic document designed to benefit the few at the expense of the many. In state after state, the Anti-Federalists reduced the issue to these social terms that the Federalists themselves had created. The Constitution, they charged, was "a continual exertion of the *well-born* of America to obtain that darling domination which they have not been able to accomplish in their respective states."[26]

The offices of the new government, the Anti-Federalists said, were "too high and exalted to be filled but [by] the *first Men* in the State in point of Fortune and Influence," while ordinary, local-minded men were to be excluded from national politics.[27] "Every man of reflection," wrote the "Federal Farmer," who was most likely the petty merchant Melancton Smith of New York, "must see that the change now proposed, is a transfer of power from the many to the few." The opponents of the Constitution grumbled that the Federalists, "those lawyers and men of learning, and monied men, . . . talk so finely and gloss over matters so smoothly, to make us poor illiterate people swallow down the pill." The smooth-talking men expected to go to Congress, to become the "managers of this Constitution, and to "get all the power and all the money into their own hands." Then they would "swallow up all us little folks, like the great *Leviathan* . . . yes, just as the whale swallowed up *Jonah*."[28] What was needed in government, said Melancton Smith, who had no college education but more than held his own in the debates in the New York convention with Alexander Hamilton and Robert R. Livingston, King's College (later Columbia) graduates, was "a suffi-cient number of the middling class," who "tended to be more tem-perate, of better morals, and less ambitious," to offset and control the "few and great."[29]

The Scotch-Irish backcountry man William Findley also gave as good as he got in the debates in the Pennsylvania conven-tion. Although the Federalists in the Pennsylvania convention overwhelmed the opponents of the Constitution and used ham-handed techniques to prevent the Anti-Federalists from being heard, Findley made himself felt. He even had a small victory in embarrassing his intellectually formidable opponents. When he claimed during the debate that Sweden lost its freedom when it lost its jury trials, the Federalists, in particular Thomas McKean, the state's chief justice, and James Wilson, the celebrated lawyer and a graduate of St. Andrews, mocked him and laughingly denied that Sweden had ever had jury trials. When the Pennsylvania convention reassembled following the Sabbath, Findley produced evidence that there had indeed been jury trials in Sweden, citing especially the third volume of William Blackstone's *Commentaries on the Laws of England*, every lawyer's bible. McKean had the good sense to remain quiet, but Wilson could not. "I do not pretend to remember every-thing I read," he sneered. "But I will add, sir, that those whose stock of knowledge is limited to a few items may easily remember and refer to them; but many things may be overlooked and forgotten in a magazine of literature." He ended by reminding Findley of the famous put-down by the notable seventeenth-century English bar-rister Sir John Maynard, of "a petulant student who reproached him with an ignorance of a trifling point: 'Young man, I have forgotten more law than ever you learned.'"[30]

No wonder the opponents of the Constitution resented Wilson's arrogance; they thought he conceived himself to be "born of a dif-ferent race from the rest of the sons of men."[31] The little exchange between Findley and Wilson was a microcosm of the social divi-sion revealed in many of the ratifying conventions, especially in the North.

In addition to seeing the Constitution as a vehicle of aristocracy, the Anti-Federalists raised the fear of what they called "consolida-tion"—that the federal government would eventually overwhelm the states and reduce them to nonentities. The Anti-Federalists invoked the doctrine of sovereignty that had been raised in the imperial debate in the 1760s and '70s. That doctrine held that there had to be in every state, one final, supreme, indivisible lawmaking power, and because of the supremacy clause, the Anti-Federalist claimed, that sovereignty would necessarily end up in the federal government. In time, the states would be diminished, involved only in trivialities—the laying out of roads and the measuring of fence posts. There was no alternative: either the federal government would absorb all power unto itself or the states would remain independent and sovereign as they were under the Articles. There was no possibility of dividing sovereignty; that would create an *imperium* in *imperio*, a power within a power. As Americans had learned from the debate with Great Britain, two supreme authorities could not exist in the same state.

It was a formidable argument, and the Federalists were hard pressed to answer it. At first, like the American patriots in the 1760s and '70s, the defenders of the Constitution tried to deny the doctrine of sovereignty. They claimed that power could be divided between the national government and the state governments. The federal government had some specific powers and the states had all the rest. This was the same argument the colonists had tried to make in the 1760s: that Parliament could regulate their trade, but it could not tax them. But the Anti-Federalists, as William Knox and Thomas Hutchinson had done in the 1760s and '70s, threw the powerful doctrine of sovereignty in their faces. Since there had to be in every state one final supreme lawmaking authority, there was no alternative: either Americans had to accept the total authority of the new Congress or they had to deny it totally and revert back to the Articles of Confederation.

Finally, James Wilson, the haughty Scotsman, came up with a solution to break the deadlock. Like the colonists in 1774, he gave up trying to divide legislative authority and fully accepted the logic of the doctrine of sovereignty. "In all governments, whatever is their form, however they may be constituted," he declared in the Pennsylvania ratifying convention, "there must be a power established from which there is no appeal, and which is therefore called absolute, supreme, and uncontrollable. The only question," he said, "is where that power is lodged." After posing the dilemma Wilson shrewdly avoided choosing between the federal government or the states. Instead of lodging this sovereignty in either Congress or the state legislatures, he relocated it outside of both. Sovereignty in America, he said, did not reside in any institution of government, or even in all the institutions of government put together. Instead, sovereignty, the final, supreme, indivisible lawmaking authority, remained with the people themselves, the people at large. Unlike in England, in America the people were never eclipsed by representation. Wilson was not saying simply that all power was derived from the people, which was conventional wisdom for all English speakers in the eighteenth century, but that final lawmaking authority actually remained with the people. "While this doctrine is known and operates," said Wilson, "we shall have a cure for every disease."[32]

It seemed that way. In America, the word *people*, as the poet Joel Barlow noted, had assumed a new meaning, broader and deeper than what it meant in Europe. In the Old World the people remained only a portion of the society; they were the poor, the canaille, the rabble, the *miserables*, the *menu peuple*, the *Pöbel*.[33] This was not true in the new republic of the United States. In America there were no orders, no estates, and the people were no longer a fragment of the society, no longer the lowest strata in a hierarchy of strata. The people had become everything, the whole society, and they were taking on a quasi-sacred character.

Wilson's notion of vesting sovereignty in the people thus seemed totally intelligible and sensible. As the idea spread through the country, the Federalists could scarcely restrain their enthusiasm in drawing out its implications—implications that had been inherent in the concept of actual representation from the beginning. In order to justify the radical constitutional changes they were making, the supporters of the Constitution began arguing that all parts of all the state governments as well as the federal government, the senates as well as the executives, were just different kinds of representatives of the people. The people retained ultimate sovereignty and doled out bits and pieces of their sovereign power to their different representatives and agents at the both the state and national levels. As Wilson in particular recognized, locating sovereignty in the people themselves makes possible the idea of federalism. The people were everywhere in all the governments, and the houses of representatives lost their once exclusive role of speaking for the people. Except for John Adams, American theorists ceased talking about politics in the way Europeans since Aristotle had—as the balancing and maneuvering of social estates. The Federalists created not just the Constitution but an entirely new intellectual world of politics.

Despite considerable opposition in many of the states to the Constitution, its eventual ratification seemed almost inevitable. Often the critics of the Constitution were unable to make their voices heard. They had fewer newspapers than the Federalists, and, as one Connecticut Anti-Federalist complained, "they were browbeaten by many of those Cicero'es as they think themselves and others of Superior rank."[34]

Besides, the Articles of Confederation were defunct; the old Congress of the Confederation had ceased meeting and it seemed inconceivable that it could be reassembled. The alternative to the Constitution seemed to be governmental chaos or the breakup of the United States into several confederations. Many who wanted to keep the Union but not the Constitution found themselves forced, as Richard Henry Lee complained, to accept "this or nothing."[35]

Most of the small states—Delaware, New Jersey, Connecticut, and Georgia—commercially dependent on their neighbors or militarily exposed, ratified immediately. The critical struggles took place in the large states of Massachusetts, Virginia, and New York. These states accepted the Constitution by only narrow margins and the promise of future amendments.

North Carolina and Rhode Island rejected the Constitution, but after New York's ratification in July 1788 the country was ready to go ahead without them. The New York ratification illustrates the Anti-Federalists' dilemma. Melancton Smith was the most vigorous and articulate of the opponents of the Constitution in the New York ratifying convention, but in the end he voted for it. His fear of disunion eventually overcame his fear of the consolidation and aristocracy that he believed the Constitution portended.

It soon became obvious to some of the Federalists that the omission of a bill of rights—a declaration of individual rights against the government—made the Constitution very vulnerable to criticism. Bills of rights had been included in many of the Revolutionary state constitutions, and the federal Constitution's lack of such a declaration of rights seemed a grave political error. Consequently, some Federalists in the state ratifying conventions promised to work for some amendments, including a bill of rights, once the Constitution was fully approved. Although Jefferson in France gave a qualified approval of the new government, he was upset that it did not include a bill of rights. "A bill of rights," he told Madison, "is what the people are entitled to against every government on earth, general or particular, and what no just government should refuse or rest on inference."

Actually, the Philadelphia Convention had scarcely discussed a bill of rights. Only during the final moments of the Convention did George Mason, the author of the Virginia declaration of rights, bring up the issue, and it was voted down by every state delegation. Most Federalists thought that a national government of specifically delegated powers made a traditional bill of rights irrelevant. But the extent of Anti-Federalist concern for this omission combined with Jefferson's public stand in favor of a bill of rights eventually forced the Federalists to give way.

Living in monarchical France, Jefferson could appreciate threats to liberty coming only from arrogant kings. So he was upset and embarrassed at the absence of a bill of rights in the new Constitution, especially since Lafayette and his other liberal French friends expected such a protection of the people's liberties against power. "The enlightened part of Europe," he told his fellow Americans, "have given us the greatest credit for inventing this instrument of security for the rights of the people, and have been not a little surprised to see us so soon give it up."[36]

Madison responded to Jefferson in October 1788. He denied that he had ever really opposed a bill of rights; he just didn't think such "parchment barriers" were very important. He conceded rather halfheartedly that a bill of rights "might be of use, and if properly executed could not be of disservice." Besides, "it is so anxiously desired by others." But then he went on with one of his usual perceptive and probing analyses of politics in an effort to explain why he had originally been reluctant to back a bill of rights. Such bills of rights in the state constitutions had not been very effective in protecting the people's liberties. In addition, writing out the rights might actually limit them. He was especially concerned with the rights of conscience, which "if submitted to public definition would be narrowed much more than they are likely ever to be by an assumed power."

But then he proceeded to put the issue in its proper context and to explain to his friend that the classical theories of politics were no longer applicable in America. He told Jefferson that he appreciated the "tendency in all Governments to an augmentation of power at the expense of liberty." The power of the one and the few had always posed a threat to the liberty of the many. But this was not the problem in republican America at that moment. "Wherever the real power in a Government lies," he said, "there is the danger of oppression. In our Government the real power lies in the majority of the Community, and the invasion of private rights is *chiefly* to be apprehended, not from acts of Government contrary to the sense of its constituents, but from acts in which the Government is the mere instrument of the major number of the constituents." There was no doubt, said Madison, that magisterial or executive "power, when it has attained a certain degree of energy and independence goes on generally to further degrees" and to become despotic and subvert liberty. Then a bill of rights protecting the people's rights made sense. "But when below that degree," which was the present situation in republican America with its weak state governors, "the direct tendency is to further degrees of relaxation, until the abuses of liberty begat a sudden transition to an undue degree of power." Too much democracy—licentiousness, in other words—led not to anarchy, as the classical theorists had predicted, but to a new and unprecedented kind of popular power or tyranny. The United States, he said, had little to fear from the classic abuse of power by the few over the many. "It is much more to be dreaded that the few will be unnecessarily sacrificed to the many."[37]

Still, bills of rights, said Madison, might have some use in a popular government. By declaring political truths in a solemn manner, they could eventually become part of the nation's culture, and they could be invoked on those rare occasions when the government is out of touch with the community.

As the leader in the new House of Representatives that convened in the spring of 1789, Madison immediately sought to fulfill the promise that he had made to support a bill of rights. He shrewdly beat back the Anti-Federalists' efforts to use their amendments to fundamentally change the structure of the Constitution and instead extracted from the variety of suggested amendments those that were least likely to drain energy from the new government. To the disappointment of many Anti-Federalists, the bill of rights— the ten amendments that were ratified in 1791—were mostly concerned with protecting from the federal government the rights of individuals rather than the rights of the states. No wonder the Anti-Federalists complained that the final bill of rights was simply "a tub to the whale," a mere diversion designed to save the main structure of the ship of state.[38]

Only the Tenth Amendment, which reserved to the states or the people those powers not delegated to the United States, was a concession to the main Anti-Federalist fear the federal government would swallow up the states. Thus, even the bill of rights that had begun as an Anti-Federalist weapon ended up being effectively wielded by the Federalists.

But the Anti-Federalists' day was coming. They had a deep and abiding fear of political power, and in 1801 they would elect a popular leader as president who would implement much of what they had wanted.

Chapter 5

Slavery and Constitutionalism

During the heated debate in the Constitutional Convention over proportional representation in the upper house of the Congress, James Madison tried to suggest that the real division in the Convention was not between the large and small states but between the slaveholding and the non-slaveholding states. Yet every delegate sensed that this was a tactical feint, designed by Madison to get the Convention off the large–small state division that was undermining his desperate effort to establish proportional representation in both houses.

It was a shrewd move, since Madison knew that slavery was a major problem for the Convention. The American Revolution had made it a problem for all Americans. Although some conscience-stricken Quakers began criticizing the institution in the middle decades of the eighteenth century, it was the Revolution that galvanized and organized their efforts and produced the first major solution to that problem. In fact, the Revolution created the first antislavery movement in the history of the world. In 1775 the first antislavery convention known to humanity met in Philadelphia at the very time the Second Continental Congress was contemplating a break from Great Britain. The Revolution and antislavery were entwined and developed together.[1]

Hereditary chattel slavery—one person owning the life and labor of another person and that person's progeny—is virtually incomprehensible to those living in the West today, even though as many as twenty-seven million people in the world may be presently enslaved.[2] In fact, slavery has existed in a variety of cultures for thousands of years, including those of the ancient Greeks and Romans, the medieval Koreans, the Pacific Northwest Indians, and the pre-Columbian Aztecs. The pre-Norman English practiced slavery, as did the ancient Vikings, the many ethnic groups of Africa, and the early Islamic Arabs; indeed, beginning in the 600s Muslims may have transported over the next twelve centuries as many sub-Saharan Africans to various parts of the Islamic world, from Spain to India, as were taken to the Western Hemisphere.[3]

Yet, as ubiquitous as slavery was in the ancient and pre-modern worlds, including the early Islamic world, there was nothing anywhere quite like the African plantation slavery that developed in the Americas. Between 1500 and the mid-nineteenth century, at least eleven or twelve million slaves were brought from Africa to the Americas. Much of the prosperity of the European colonies in the New World depended upon the labor of these millions of African slaves and their enslaved descendants. Slavery existed everywhere in the Americas, from the villages of French Canada to the sugar plantations of Portuguese Brazil.

Slavery in the British North American mainland differed greatly from the slavery in the rest of the New World. In the course of the seventeenth and eighteenth centuries the English mainland colonies imported three to four hundred thousand African slaves, a very small percentage of the millions that were brought to the Caribbean and South American colonies, where the mortality rates were horrendous. Far fewer slaves died prematurely in the North American mainland. In fact, by the late eighteenth century the slaves in most of the English mainland colonies were reproducing at the same rates as whites, already among the most fertile peoples in the Western world.

Like people everywhere in premodern societies, most American colonists initially took slavery for granted, felt no guilt over it, and simply accepted it as the lowest and meanest rank in a complicated hierarchy of dependencies and statuses of unfreedom. By 1819 John Adams knew that slavery was no longer considered normal and acceptable in the way it had been before the Revolution. He recalled that in colonial Massachusetts sixty or so years earlier the owning of slaves "was not disgraceful," and "the best men in my Vicinity— thought it not inconsistent with their Characters."[4] With half of colonial society at any one moment legally unfree—that is, lacking the capacity to engage in civic life, to marry, to travel, to own property, and liable at any time to be bought and sold—the peculiar character of lifetime, hereditary black slavery was not always as obvious to colonial gentry elites as it would become during the Revolutionary movement.

To many slaveholders and other elites in the colonial period, black slavery often seemed indistinguishable from the unfreedom of white servitude. Bonded servants were everywhere in the colonies, especially in the middle and northern colonies. As late as 1759 Benjamin Franklin thought that indentured servants brought from Britain, Ireland, and Germany were performing most of the labor of the middle colonies. In fact, one-half to two-thirds of the white immigrants to the colonies came as indentured servants. Among these immigrants there were an estimated 50,000 British and Irish convicts and vagabonds shipped to America between 1718 and 1775 and bound over as servants for periods of seven or fourteen years, or in some cases even for life.[5]

Of course, white servitude was rarely for life and was never hereditary; nevertheless, bonded servitude in North America was a much harsher, more brutal, and more humiliating status than it was in England. For that reason, colonial bonded servitude shared some of the dependent nature of black slavery—though not the blackness that English culture from the sixteenth century had associated with night, the devil, and evil.[6] Although white servants were members of their master's household and enjoyed some legal rights, their contracts were a kind of property that could be bought and sold. Colonial servants were not simply young people drawn from the lowest social ranks but, more commonly, indentured immigrants who had sold their labor in order to get to the New World. Precisely because these imported servants were expensive, their indentures or contracts were written, and their terms of service were longer than those of English servants—five to seven years rather than the yearlong oral agreements typical in England.[7]

Because labor was so valuable in America, the colonists enacted numerous laws designed to control the movement of white servants and to prevent runaways. There was nothing in England resembling the passes required in all the colonies for traveling servants. As expensive labor, most colonial servants or their contracts could be bought and sold, rented out, seized for the debts of their masters, and conveyed in wills to heirs. Colonial servants often belonged to their masters in ways that English servants did not. They could not marry, buy or sell property, or leave their households without their master's permission. Those convicted of crimes were often bound over for one or more years to their victims who could use or sell their labor.[8]

No wonder newly arriving Britons were astonished to see how ruthlessly Americans treated their white servants. "Generally speaking," said royal official William Eddis upon his introduction to Maryland society in 1769, "they groan beneath a burden worse than Egyptian bondage." Eddis even thought that black slaves were better treated than white servants.[9] But in this cruel, premodern, pre-humanitarian world, better treatment of the lower orders was quite relative. Superiors took their often brutal and fierce treatment of inferiors as part of the nature of things and not something out of the ordinary—not in a society where the life of the lowly seemed cheap. Even the most liberal of masters could coolly and callously describe the savage punishments they inflicted on their black slaves. "I tumbled him into the Sellar," wrote Virginia planter Landon Carter in his diary, "and there had him tied Neck and heels all night and this morning had him stripped and tied up to a limb."[10] But whites among the mean and lowly could be treated harshly too. In the 1770s a drunken and abusive white servant being taken to Virginia was horsewhipped, put in irons and thumb-screwed, and then handcuffed and gagged for a night; he remained handcuffed for at least nine days.[11]

All those who were dependent and unfree had much in common. As late as the 1750s immigrant redemptioners, as one observer noted, were being bought in parcels at Philadelphia and driven in tens and twenties "like cattle to a Smithfield market and exposed to sale in public fairs as so many brute beasts." Like black slaves, white servants too could be advertised for sale as "choice" and "well-disposed."[12]

Because the subjugation of colonial servitude was so much harsher and more conspicuous than it was in England, it was sometimes difficult for colonial elites to perceive the distinctive peculiarity of black slavery. Slavery often seemed to be just another degree of unfreedom, another degree of labor, more severe and more abject, to be sure, but not in the eyes of many colonial gentry all that different from white servitude and white labor. Both kinds of servants shared the contempt in which manual labor traditionally was held, and both were plainly dependent in a world that valued only independence. Slaves were often described simply as another kind of dependent in the patriarchal family composed of many dependents. "Next to our children and brethren by blood," said Reverend Thomas Bacon of Maryland in 1743, "our servants, and especially our slaves, are certainly in the nearest relation to us. They are an immediate and necessary part of our households." Thus, black slaves and white servants were often lumped together as dependents. William Byrd in his diary mentioned about fifty servants by name, but he rarely differentiated between black and white servants; when he did so, it was only to distinguish between two servants bearing the same name. In colonial Virginia black slaves and lowly whites mingled with one another in horse racing and cockfighting sites and in churches much more frequently than they would following the Revolution. Still, the existence of slavery and servitude everywhere bred a pervasive sense of hierarchy where some were free and independent and the rest were unfree and dependent.[13]

The Revolution changed everything: unfreedom could no longer be taken for granted as a normal part of a hierarchical society. Almost overnight black slavery and white servitude became conspicuous and reviled in ways that they had not been earlier. Under the pressure of the imperial debate the Revolutionaries tended to collapse the many degrees of dependency of the social hierarchy into two simple distinctions and thus brought into stark relief the anomalous nature of all dependencies. If a person wasn't free and independent, then he had to be a servant or slave. Since the radical Whig writers, from whom the colonists drew many of their ideas, tended to divide society into just two parts, the *"Freemen,"* who in John Toland's words, were "men of property, or persons that are able to live of themselves," and the dependent, "those who cannot subsist in this independence, I call *Servants,"* it was natural during the imperial crisis for the colonists to apply this same dichotomy to themselves.[14] If they were to accept the Stamp Act and other parliamentary legislation, they would become dependent on English whims and thus become slaves.

Suddenly the debate between Great Britain and its colonies made any form of dependency equal to slavery. "What is a slave," asked a New Jersey writer in 1765, "but one who depends upon the will of another for the enjoyment of his life and property?" "Liberty," said Stephen Hopkins of Rhode Island, quoting the seventeenth-century radical Whig Algernon Sidney, "solely consists in an independency upon the will of another; and by the name of slave, we understand a man who can neither dispose of his person or goods, but enjoys all at the will of his master." If Americans did not resist the Stamp Act, said Hopkins, slaves were precisely what they would become. In 1775 John Adams drew the ultimate conclusion and posed the social dichotomy about as starkly as possible. "There are," said Adams simply, "but two sorts of men in the world, freemen and slaves."[15]

This sharp dichotomy made white servitude impossible to sustain. If all dependencies, including servitude, were to be equated with slavery, then white male servants balked at their status and increasingly refused to enter into any indentures. They knew the difference between servitude and slavery. If they had to be servants, they wanted to be called "help," and they refused to call their employers "master" or "mistress." Instead, many substituted the term "boss," derived from the Dutch term for master. By 1775 in Philadelphia the proportion of the work force that was unfree—composed of servants and slaves—had already declined to 13 percent from the 40–50 percent that it had been at mid-century. By 1800 less than 2 percent of the city's labor force remained unfree. Before long, for all intents and purposes, indentured white servitude disappeared everywhere in America.[16]

The rapid decline of servitude made black slavery more conspicuous than it had been before—its visibility heightened by its black racial character. Suddenly, the only unfree people in the society were black slaves, and for many, including many of the slaves themselves, this was an anomaly that had to be dealt with. However deeply rooted and however racially prejudiced white Americans were, slavery could not remain immune to challenge in this new world that was celebrating freedom and independency as never before.

Although everyone knew that eliminating slavery would be far more difficult than ridding the country of servitude, there were moments of optimism, even in the South. For the first time in American history the owning of slaves was put on the defensive. The colonists didn't need Dr. Samuel Johnson's jibe in 1775— "how come we hear the loudest yelps for liberty from the drivers of Negroes?"—to remind them of the obvious contradiction between their libertarian rhetoric and their owning of slaves.[17] "The Colonists are by the law of nature free born," declared James Otis of Massachusetts in his 1764 pamphlet, "as indeed all men are, white or black." Otis went on to challenge the owning of slaves and the practice of the slave trade and to point out that "those who barter away other men's liberty will soon care little for their own."[18]

Not all Americans who criticized slavery were as frank and spirited as Otis, but everyone who thought himself enlightened became uneasy over slavery in his midst. Even some of the southern planters became troubled by their ownership of slaves. This was especially true in the colony of Virginia.

In 1766 a young Thomas Jefferson was elected to Virginia's House of Burgesses, where, as he says in his autobiography, he introduced a measure for the emancipation of slaves in the colony. His colleagues rejected the measure, but they did not reject Jefferson, who soon became one of the most important members of the legislature. By the time he wrote his instructions to the Virginia delegation to the First Continental Congress, immediately published as *A Summary View of the Rights of British America* (1774), he openly voiced his opposition to the "infamous" slave trade and declared that "the abolition of domestic slavery is the great object of desire in these colonies where it was unhappily introduced in their infant state."[19]

Many of Jefferson's Virginia colleagues, equally uncomfortable with their slaveholding, were gradually coming to think differently about the future of the institution. They sensed that they had too many slaves already, and they thus became increasingly sympathetic to ending the despicable overseas slave trade. Tobacco had exhausted the soil, and many planters, including George Washington, had turned to growing wheat, which did not require the same human labor as tobacco production. Consequently, more and more slaveholders had begun hiring out their slaves to employers in Richmond and Norfolk. This suggested to many that slavery might eventually be replaced by wage labor. Some Virginians hoped that the impending break from Great Britain might allow them not only to end the slave trade but to end the colony's prohibition against manumissions.[20]

Although at least one historian has claimed that the Somerset decision of 1772 "caused a sensation in the colonies," prominent Virginian slaveholders paid little attention to it, even though the decision was soon published in a Virginia newspaper.[21] Landon Carter never mentioned the decision in his diary. Neither did Jefferson and Washington or their many correspondents allude to the Somerset case in their many exchanges of letters. The same was true of Virginia's leading Revolutionaries Richard Henry Lee, Edmund Pendleton, and George Mason; although all were substantial slaveholders, none commented on the Somerset decision in his letters.

James Somerset, a slave of Charles Steuart, a Virginia official, had run off when his master was visiting London. After being
captured, Somerset, with the aid of Granville Sharp and other
British abolitionists, sued for his freedom. Lord Mansfield, chief
justice of the King's Bench, freed Somerset, stating that slavery required positive law for its existence, and since no such law existed
in England, Somerset could not be enslaved.[22] This was a narrowly
argued decision, and it had no application to the colonies; indeed,
no colonial official in North America took notice of the decision.[23]

But black slaves were aware of the decision. Backed by antislavery advocates in the northern colonies, they picked it up and,
especially in Massachusetts, sued for their freedom. In Virginia,
however, there was little objection to the decision, which was not
really contrary to the sentiments of many of Virginia's enlightened
slaveholding planters. In fact, the article in the *Virginia Gazette*
that announced the Somerset decision mocked the logic of color-
based slavery, declaring that "if Negroes are to be slaves on Account
of Colour, the next step will be to enslave every Mulatto in the
Kingdom, then all the Portuguese, then the brown complexioned
English, and so on till there be only one Free Man left, which will
be the Man of the palest Complexion in the three Kingdoms."[24] At
the time of the Revolution at least some Virginians did not believe
that all blacks had to be slaves, and many others were anything but
fearful of antislavery. In 1791 the board of visitors of the College of
William and Mary, slaveholders all, awarded an honorary degree to
Granville Sharp, the leading British abolitionist at the time.

All these developments in Virginia made the possibility of
ending slavery seem increasingly realistic, which in turn led to the
emergence of a growing number of antislavery societies in the Upper
South—more even than in the North. If Virginians, dominating the
North American colonies as they did, could conceive of an end to

slavery, or least an end of the dreadful slave trade, then many other Americans could see the possibility of entering a new enlightened antislavery era—an era that would coincide with their break from Great Britain.[25]

Nearly everywhere there was a mounting sense that slavery was on its last legs and was dying a natural death. On the eve of the Revolution Dr. Benjamin Rush of Pennsylvania believed that the desire to abolish the institution "prevails in our counsels and among the all ranks in every province." With opposition to slavery growing throughout the Atlantic world, he predicted in 1774 that "there will be not a Negro slave in North America in 40 years."[26]

Rush and the many others who made the same predictions could not, of course, have been more wrong. They lived with illusions, illusions fed by the anti-slave sentiments spreading in Virginia and elsewhere in the northern colonies. Far from dying, slavery was on the verge of its greatest expansion. There were more slaves in the United States at the end of the Revolutionary era than at the beginning.

Because Virginia possessed two hundred thousand slaves, over 40 percent of the nearly five hundred thousand African American slaves who existed in all the North American colonies, its influence dominated and skewed the attitudes of many other colonists. Farther south, there was another, much harsher reality.

Both South Carolina, with about seventy-five thousand slaves, and Georgia, with about twenty thousand, had no sense whatsoever of having too many slaves. For them slavery seemed to be just getting underway. Planters in these deep southern states had no interest whatsoever in manumitting their slaves and in fact were eager to expand the overseas importation of slaves. If only other Americans paid attention, they would have realized that the Carolinians and Georgians would brook no outside interference with their property in slaves. Washington knew this, which is why he claimed that South Carolina and Georgia were the only really "Southern states" in the Union. Virginia, he said, was not part of the South at all, but was one of "the middle states," not all that different from Pennsylvania, New Jersey, and New York.[27]

By the end of 1774 Virginia and the other colonies had already become independent in fact. Royal governors looked on in amazement as their authority slipped away, to be replaced from below by local governments composed of committees of various sorts. Lord Dunmore, royal governor of Virginia, like most royal governors, fled from the Revolutionary mobs to the safety of a British warship. He was desperate for military support to put down the rebels, and in early November 1775 he issued a proclamation promising freedom to fugitive servants and slaves who were willing to join His Majesty's troops. In the following weeks hundreds of slaves fled to Dunmore's Ethiopian Regiment. By the end of the Revolutionary War it is estimated that about twenty thousand black slaves joined the British side, with roughly twelve thousand coming from the South. It was one of the great liberations prior to the Civil War.[28]

Dunmore's Proclamation infuriated the Virginia slaveholders and prompted those few Virginians who were still hesitant to finally join the rebel cause. Virginia was one of the most radical colonies, containing, except for the Anglican clergy, very few loyalists. Well before Dunmore's Proclamation of November 1775, the colony was more than ready to break from Britain; fear of losing its slaves had nothing to do with its highly concerted move toward independence.[29]

The Continental Congress, which met in 1774, urged the colonies to abolish the slave trade. Jefferson believed that the British Crown was responsible for the slave trade, but in drafting the Declaration of Independence he discovered that blaming George

III for its horrors was too much for his colleagues in the Congress. South Carolina and Georgia objected to the accusation, he later explained, and even some northern delegates were "a little tender" on the issue, "for though their people have very few slaves themselves yet they had been pretty considerable carriers."[30]

With independence, nearly all the newly independent states, including Virginia, began moving against slavery, initiating what became the first great antislavery movement in world history. The desire to abolish slavery was not an incidental offshoot of the Revolution; it was not an unintended consequence of the contagion of liberty. It was part and parcel of the many enlightened reforms that were integral to the republican revolutions taking place in the new states. The abolition of slavery was as important as the other major reforms the states undertook: their disestablishment of the Church of England, their plans for public education, their changes in the laws of inheritance, and their codification of the common law, and their transformation of criminal punishment.

Of course, many of these enlightened plans and hopes went unfulfilled or were postponed for later generations to accomplish; that was certainly the fate of the many elaborate plans for creating systems of public education. But despite flying in the face of the rights of property that were sacred to the ideology of the Revolution, the abolition of slavery was remarkably successful, at least in the northern states.

Although nearly 90 percent of all the slaves lived in the South, northern colonists possessed nearly fifty thousand slaves, a not inconsequential number. In 1767 nearly 9 percent of the population of Philadelphia was enslaved. In the middle of the eighteenth century one out of every five families in Boston owned at least one slave. In 1760 black slaves made up nearly 8 percent of the population of Rhode Island, 7 percent of the population of New Jersey, and 14 percent of the city of New York. It was not just the southern Revolutionary leaders—Washington, Jefferson, Madison, and so on—who owned slaves; so did many of the northern leaders— Boston's John Hancock, New York's Robert Livingston, and Philadelphia's John Dickinson were slaveholders. On the eve of the Revolution the mayor of Philadelphia possessed thirty-one slaves. Yet the northern colonies were not slave societies, like those of the South, and the slaves were recognized in law as human beings, not chattel, as they were in the southern courts.[31]

Although modern historians express frustration with the slowness and ragged nature of the Revolutionaries' struggles to end slavery in the states, the fact that it had been legal everywhere in colonial North America and had existed for millennia throughout the world make the scale and the unprecedented nature of the antislavery movements in the new republics look relatively impressive. Looking back from our present perspective, we find the states' antislavery efforts to be puny, partial, and disappointing, but from the perspective of colonial society in, say, 1720 when slavery existed everywhere without substantial challenge, the Revolutionary achievement that began a half century later appears extraordinary and exciting. This move to end slavery was brought about by the efforts of many blacks as well as whites.

As early as 1774 Rhode Island and Connecticut ended the importation of African slaves into their colonies. In the preamble to their law the Rhode Islanders declared that since "the inhabitants of America are generally engaged in the preservations of their own rights and liberties, among which that of personal freedom must be considered the greatest," it was obvious that "those who are desirous of enjoying all the advantages of liberty themselves should be willing to extend personal liberty to others."[32] Other states— Delaware, Virginia, Maryland, and South Carolina—soon followed in abolishing the slave trade; South Carolina, however, only for a term of years.

With independence Americans began attacking slavery itself. In 1777 the people of Vermont, in hopes of soon joining the new United States as the fourteenth state, drew up a constitution. The first article of that constitution stated that because all men were "born equally free and independent," and possessed "certain natural, inherent, and unalienable rights, . . . therefore, no male person, born in this country, or brought from over sea, ought to be holden by law, to serve any person, as a servant, slave, or apprentice, after he arrives to the age of twenty-one years; nor female, in like manner, after she arrives to the age of eighteen years, unless they are bound by their own consent."[33]

This article of the Vermont constitution linked the abolition of slavery to the enlightened ideals of the Revolution as explicitly and as closely as one could imagine. It also revealed how Americans thought about slavery in relation to other forms of unfreedom existing in colonial America. Although the article was not rigidly enforced, and slavery and other forms of unfreedom continued to linger on in Vermont, it nevertheless represented a remarkable moment in the history of the New World.

In 1780 Pennsylvania passed an act for the gradual abolition of slavery, stating that "all Persons, as well Negroes, and Mulattos, as others, who shall be brought within this State, from and after the Passing of this Act, shall not be deemed and considered as Servants for Life or Slaves."[34] The statute did not, however, free the six thousand or so slaves already living in the state, and children born to slave mothers had to serve as indentured servants until age twenty-eight. The attorneys for the state's antislavery society often found it politically useful to identify the status of slaves with that of servants, "for there is no Difference or Distinction between Temporary

Servants—Whether White or Black—on Account of the length of time they have to serve."[35] By 1790 there were less than four thousand slaves left in the state, together with about ten thousand free blacks.

In Massachusetts free and enslaved blacks had been using the courts as early as 1764 to gain their freedom. Increasingly juries found against the masters and in favor of the slaves. In 1781 Chief Justice William Cushing of the state's supreme court told a jury that "the holding of Africans in perpetual servitude and sell and buy them as we do our horses and cattle" may have been countenanced by the laws of the province but "nowhere is it expressly enacted or established." With independence, he said, a "different idea has taken place with the people of America, more favorable to the natural rights of mankind." In a subsequent case in 1783 Cushing was more emphatic, declaring that by the new Massachusetts constitution of 1780, "slavery is . . . as effectively abolished as it can be by the granting of rights and privileges wholly incompatible and repugnant to its existence."[36]

Although Massachusetts used the courts to end slavery, Connecticut and Rhode Island passed laws gradually abolishing slavery in the way Vermont had, by making all children born after a certain date apprentices until age twenty-one in the case of males, and eighteen in the case of females. New Hampshire had so few slaves that slavery died away without the need for legislative or judicial action.

In the middle states of New York and New Jersey, abolition was much more difficult. In 1781 New York offered to pay slaveholders for assigning their slaves to the Revolutionary forces and the promise of freedom for the slaves at the end of the war. Although by the 1790s only one in three blacks in New York City was free, the state was slow to attack the institution. In 1799 the state legislature declared that children of slaves born after July 4, 1799, would be legally free, but they would have to serve as indentured servants until age twenty-eight for males, and twenty-five for females. All the existing slaves in the state had their status redefined as indentured servitude for life.

New Jersey was the last northern state to abolish slavery. The law of 1804 freed all children of slaves born after July 4, 1804, with the children serving as apprentices until age twenty-five for males, and twenty-one for females. By 1830 two-thirds of the slaves still remaining in the North lived in New Jersey.

In 1787 the Confederation Congress became involved with slavery for the first time. It issued the Northwest Ordinance, which laid out a three-step process by which territories in the Northwest would become states that would be equal in all respects to the original states—an extraordinarily generous action and an important assertion of federal authority. In 1789 the new Congress elected under the Constitution renewed the document and made it part of national law. Article 6 of the Ordinance provided that "there shall be neither slavery nor involuntary servitude in the said territory, otherwise than in the punishment of crimes whereof the party shall have been duly convicted."[37] Abraham Lincoln later used the Ordinance to bolster his claim that the federal government had authority to forbid the extension of slavery into the territories. Indeed, as has been nicely pointed out, Lincoln put together a structure of "antislavery constitutionalism"; he joined the Ordinance with the Declaration of Independence and the Constitution into a bundle of founding texts "that convincingly positioned the antislavery argument within the boundaries of the American system."[38]

By the early nineteenth century all the northern states had provided for the eventual end of slavery, and Congress had promised the creation of free states in the Northwest Territory. By 1790s the number of free blacks in the northern states had increased from several hundred in the 1770s to over twenty-seven thousand. By 1810 there were well over one hundred thousand free blacks in the North. For a moment it looked as the institution of slavery might be rolled back everywhere.

The Upper South began to move against slavery, which reinforced the idea that the institution's days were numbered. In 1782 the Virginia legislature allowed individual slaveholders to manumit their slaves without legislative approval. Delaware and Maryland soon followed with similar laws. In Virginia and Maryland antislavery societies brought "freedom suits" in the state courts that led to some piecemeal emancipation. If the slaves could demonstrate to the courts that they had maternal Indian ancestors, they could be freed, and hearsay evidence was often enough to convince the courts. "Whole families," recalled one sympathetic observer, "were often liberated by a single verdict, the fate of one relative deciding the fate of many." By 1796 nearly thirty freedom suits were pending in Virginia courts.[39] Some slaves took advantage of the new liberal laws and worked to buy their own freedom. Of the slaves freed in Norfolk, Virginia, between 1791 and 1820, more than a third purchased themselves or were purchased by others, usually by their families. By 1790 the free black population in the Upper South had increased to over thirty thousand; by 1810 the free blacks in the area numbered over ninety-four thousand. The growing numbers of free blacks in the Upper South convinced many that the institution of slavery was indeed dying.

John Melish, a British traveler in the South in 1806, declared that nearly every person he met condemned slavery, generally expressing the opinion that it was "not only hurtful to public morals, but contrary to every maxim of sound policy." Yet Melish realized that slavery in the southern states was "incorporated with the whole system of civil society; its influence has extended through every branch of domestic economy; and to do it away must be a work of time." That was the hope of many—that time would end the institution.[40]

Although the Virginians' efforts to end slavery convinced many that the North and South were becoming more alike, other, more realistic observers knew better. Stephen Higginson, a worldly Boston merchant, was convinced in 1785 that "in their habits, manners and commercial Interests, the southern and northern States are not only very dissimilar, but in many instances directly opposed."[41] When the delegates to the Constitutional Convention gathered in Philadelphia in 1787 those differences quickly became apparent.

Although the northern delegates, even those seriously opposed to slavery, did not come to the Convention intending to use the framing of a new constitution as a means of abolishing slavery in the South, they certainly realized that the two sections had very different economic interests and therefore the allotment of power between the northern and southern states in the new government was important. Thus, when Madison at the outset of the Convention objected to a proposal to base representation in the House solely on "the number of free inhabitants," the northern delegates knew immediately that the southern states would want some kind of representation of their slaves in the new government. The debate over the allocation of representatives in the House consumed over six weeks of debate, from late May until mid-July.[42]

Essentially the delegates from the South sought to have wealth or property taken into account in representation in the proposed Congress; in fact, the members from the states of the Deep South wanted their slaves to count equally with whites in allotting representation. By contrast, northern delegates urged that slaves not count at all. Elbridge Gerry of Massachusetts argued that if blacks as property in the South were to be counted for representation of the southern states, then the cattle and horses of the North should likewise be counted for representation of the northern states.

Although the delegates from the Upper South did not support South Carolina's position that slaves should be counted equally with whites for purposes of representation, they were not willing to have the slaves not count at all. As Madison later explained in *Federalist* No. 54, the Convention ended up treating the slaves "in the mixt character of persons and of property."[43] It fell back on a formula that the Congress had used in the Confederation period in apportioning requisitions on the states—applying it to representation as well as direct taxation: all the free white inhabitants plus three-fifths of all other persons. It seemed a necessary compromise to keep the states of the Deep South from leaving the Convention.

Thus was born the notorious three-fifths clause of the Constitution that became what many northerners came to believe was the source that allowed the "slave power" of the South to dominate the federal government in the antebellum period.[44] In 1820, during the debate over the admission of Missouri into the Union as a slave state, Rufus King, who had been a delegate from Massachusetts in the Convention, admitted in the United States Senate that "the disproportionate power and influence allowed to the slaveholding states was a necessary sacrifice to the establishment of the Constitution."[45]

The threat by South Carolina and Georgia to walk out of the Convention led to additional compromises with slavery. Although all the states except those of the Deep South were willing to end the international slave trade, the Convention had to agree to allow the continued importation of slaves for twenty years. "Great as the evil is," Madison later said in the Virginia ratifying convention, "a dismemberment of the Union would be worse."[46] The northern states also had to accept a ban on Congress's ability to tax exports, the export trade of staples being crucial to the South. Some northern delegates wanted to call the South Carolinians' and Georgians' bluff—if indeed it was a bluff. But enough delegates believed that, since slavery was naturally dying, the issue was not worth risking a breakup of the Union and destroying the opportunity to frame a new constitution. Oliver Ellsworth of Connecticut thought the whole issue was irrelevant. He predicted that "as population increases, poor laborers will be so plentiful as to render slaves useless, and thus slavery in time will not be a speck in our country."[47]

Many northerners agreed. Some even thought the Constitution worked to end slavery. Thomas Dawes Jr., a judge and a delegate from Boston to the Massachusetts ratifying convention, realized that Congress, he said, could not simply abolish slavery "in a moment, and so destroy what our Southern brethren consider as property." But he believed that Congress's ability in twenty years to abolish the slave trade, together with its immediate power to impose a duty of ten dollars on each imported slave, would eventually spell the end of slavery in the country. "As slavery is not smitten by an apoplexy" that would kill it quickly, "yet," he said, "it has received a mortal wound and will die of consumption," a slow but relentless mode of dying.[48] All these delusions about the impending end of slavery made compromising easier and prevented people from foreseeing their horrific future.

The final concession to the delegates from the Deep South had to do with the returning of fugitive slaves to their owners. Although the problem of returning escaped slaves in time became one of the rawest and most divisive issues dividing the North and South, it stirred very little controversy in the Convention, especially compared to the issues involving representation and the slave trade.

The problem arose only because the northern states had begun ending slavery, which meant that there were more and more free places to which the slaves could flee; that in itself was a measure of the success of the antislavery movement since 1776.

The southern slaveowners wanted to ensure that any slave fleeing to a free state would be returned to them. Apparently, southerners in the Confederation Congress, meeting in New York at the same time as the Philadelphia Convention, agreed to prohibit slavery in the Northwest Territory only if northerners guaranteed the lawful return of escaped slaves in both the Ordinance and the Constitution. At any rate, when the Fugitive Slave Clause (Article I, Section 2, Clause 3) was introduced in the Convention on August 29, 1787, no delegate voted against it. Within decades, this clause became the source of the bitterest northern opposition to the slaveholding South.[49]

Although the delegates had embedded all these protections for slavery in the Constitution, many of them, including Madison, did not want the Constitution explicitly to endorse slavery and to affirm in any way the notion that slaves were property. It would be wrong, Madison said in the Convention, "to admit in the Constitution the idea that there could be property in men."[50] Consequently, the Convention was scrupulous in avoiding mention of "slaves," "slavery," or "Negroes" in the final draft of the Constitution. This decision seemed to suggest that the United States would eventually be without the shameful institution of slavery.

Some abolitionists like William Lloyd Garrison who later indicted the Constitution as a "covenant with death" and "an agreement with hell" had no awareness of the context in which the Constitution had been created decades earlier.[51] Unlike Lincoln, they appreciated neither the hopes of the framers nor the importance of the Constitution to the existence of the Union. [52]

Many in 1787 hoped that slavery would not long endure. Yet the explosive proslavery response by representatives from the Deep South to two petitions to Congress from the Pennsylvania Abolition Society in 1790 to end the slave trade and slavery itself should have indicated that the eradication of slavery was not going to be as inevitable as many had hoped. "Let me remind men who expect a general emancipation by law," warned one outraged South Carolinian congressman, "that this would never be submitted to by the Southern States without civil war!" South Carolina began planning to reopen its slave trade and to bring in more slaves than it had before.[53]

Despite the worrying behavior of the states of the Deep South, many leaders, including those in the Upper South, still remained confident of the future. They were willing to table the anti-slave petitions for the sake of the Union in the mistaken hope that the Revolutionary ideals of "humanity and freedom" were, as Madison put it in 1790, "secretly undermining the institution."[54] All the noise about slavery, said Madison, could only delay but not stop the inevitable march of progress.

By the 1790s, however, there were already signs that Virginia's earlier enthusiasm for limiting slavery was dissipating. Manumissions declined and the freedom suits stopped. The Virginian slaveholders who had migrated into Kentucky were determined to protect their property. Although slaves constituted only 16 percent of Kentucky's population, the minority of slaveholders were able to write into the state's 1792 constitution a provision declaring that "the legislature shall have no power to pass laws for the emancipation of slaves without the consent of their owners." It was the nation's first explicit constitutional protection of slavery and an ominous sign of what lay ahead.[55]

Probably nothing in the 1790s changed the atmosphere in the country more than the outbreak of a black slave rebellion in the

French colony of Saint Domingue. Most Americans, including slaves, knew what was happening on the island. Between 1791 and 1804 the American press carried ever more terrifying news of atrocities on Saint Domingue, frightening slaveholders everywhere. With slave rebellions breaking out in Puerto Rico, Venezuela, Curaçao, and Grenada, southerners increasingly realized, as Governor Charles Pinckney of South Carolina declared, "that the day will arrive when [the southern states] may be exposed to the same insurrection." As talk of slave insurrections in the United States increased, "the emancipation fume," as one Virginia slaveholder put it, "has long evaporated and not a word is said about it."[56] By the end of the 1790s whatever antislavery sentiments Virginia had once possessed were gone. In 1800 the conspiracy of the free black Gabriel to launch a black rebellion in Virginia guaranteed that the state's earlier anti-slave liberalism would never be revived.

By the early decades of the nineteenth century the two sections of North and South may have been both very American and very republican, both spouting a similar rhetoric of liberty and equal rights, but below the surface they were fast becoming very different places, with different economies, different cultures, and different ideals—the northern middle-class-dominated society coming to value common manual labor as a supreme human activity, the southern planter-dominated society continuing to think of labor in traditional terms as mean and despicable and fit only for slaves.[57]

Yet that northern middle-class society had little or no grounds for celebrating its progressiveness in opposing slavery. The freedom that the North's black slaves earned in the decades following the Revolution came with some perverse consequences. Freedom for black slaves did not give them equality. Indeed, emancipation aggravated racial bigotry and inequality. As long as slavery determined the status of blacks, whites did not have think about racial discrimination and racial equality. But once black slaves were freed, race became the principal determinant of their status. Republicanism implied equal citizenship, but unfortunately, few white Americans in the post-Revolutionary decades were prepared to grant equal rights to freed blacks. Consequently, racial prejudice and racial segregation spread everywhere in the new Republic. In 1829 William Lloyd Garrison believed that "the prejudices of the north are stronger than those of the south." [58]

As the poor white man gained the right to vote in the early nineteenth-century North, the free black man lost it. By the heyday of Jacksonian democracy, popular white majorities in state after state in the North had moved to eliminate the remaining property restrictions on white voters while at the same time taking away the franchise from black voters who in some cases had exercised it for decades. In some states, like Pennsylvania, black exclusion was the price paid for lower-class whites gaining the right to vote, universal suffrage having been opposed on the grounds that it would add too many blacks to the electorate. In other states, like New York, exclusion of blacks from the franchise was an effective way for Democratic Party majorities to eliminate once and for all blocs of black voters who too often had voted first for Federalist and then for Whig candidates. Some northern states even granted the suffrage to Irish immigrants who had not yet become citizens at the same time as they took the right to vote away from blacks born and bred in the United States. No state admitted to the Union after 1819 allowed blacks to vote. By 1840, 93 percent of northern free blacks lived in states that completely or practically excluded them from the suffrage and hence from participation in politics.[59]

Despite this resultant racial segregation and exclusion and despite the often sluggish and uneven character of the abolition in the North, we should not lose sight of the immensity of what the

Revolution accomplished. For the first time in the slaveholding societies of the New World, the institution of slavery was constitutionally challenged and abolished in the northern states. It was one thing for the imperial legislatures of France and Britain to abolish slavery as they did in 1794 and 1833 in their far-off slave-ridden Caribbean colonies; but it was quite another for slaveholding states themselves to abolish the institution. For all of its faults and failures, the abolition of slavery in the northern states in the post-Revolutionary years pointed the way toward the eventual elimination of the institution throughout not just the United States but the whole of the New World.

Chapter 6

The Emergence of the Judiciary

In the massive rethinking that took place in the 1780s and 1790s nearly all parts of America's governments were reformed and reconstituted—reforms and reconstitutions that were often justified by ingenious manipulations of Montesquieu's very permissive doctrine of the "separation of powers." But the part of government that benefited most from the rethinking and remodeling of the 1780s and 1790s was the judiciary. In the decade following the Declaration of Independence the position of the judiciary in American life began to be transformed—from the much scorned and insignificant appendage of crown authority into what Americans increasingly called one of "the three capital powers of Government," from minor magistrates identified with the colonial executives into an equal and independent part of a modern tripartite government.[1]

It is difficult to recapture the peculiar character of the colonial judiciary in the decades prior to the American Revolution. The colonial judges lacked the independence of modern judges and didn't even have the independence of their counterparts in the mother country, who as a consequence of the Glorious Revolution in 1688 had won tenure during good behavior. By contrast, the colonial judges continued to hold office at the pleasure of the Crown.

Often adjudication was the least of the judges' duties. They were lesser magistrates carrying out the responsibilities of the royal governors or chief magistrates. Sitting on county courts, they not only settled disputes but handled a wide variety of "administrative" tasks, drawing on the community for help. They assessed taxes, granted licenses, oversaw poor relief, supervised road repair, set prices, upheld moral standards, and all in all monitored the localities over which they presided.

Consequently, most colonists could scarcely discern any difference of responsibility between these lesser magistrates and the chief executives, the royal governors. Indeed, some concluded that there were really "no more than two powers in any government, viz. the power to make laws, and the power to execute them; for the judicial power is only a branch of the executive, the chief of every country being the first magistrate." Even John Adams in 1766 regarded "the first grand division of constitutional powers" as "those of legislation and those of execution," with "the administration of justice" resting in "the executive part of the constitution." The colonial judges therefore bore much of the opprobrium attached to the royal governors and were often constrained and checked by the power of popular juries to an extent not found in England. Adams went out of his way to emphasize the power of the juries whose verdicts overruled all matters of law and fact, even when they were "in Direct opposition to the Direction of the Court."[2]

Since Americans had become convinced that the dependence of the judges on executive caprice and the will of the Crown was "dangerous to liberty and property of the Subject," they sought to end that dependence at the Revolution.[3] Most of the Revolutionary state constitutions of 1776–77 took away from the governors their traditional power to appoint judges and gave it to the legislatures.

The judges' tenure clearly no longer depended on the pleasure of the chief magistrate.

While the Revolution eliminated the courts' earlier dependence on the governors, it increasingly brought them under the dominion of the legislatures. Their dependence on the state legislatures was an example of the way, as Madison put it, the state assembles were drawing all power into their "impetuous vortex."[4]

Because judges had been so much identified with the hated magisterial power, many American Revolutionaries in 1776 sought not to strengthen the judiciary but to weaken it. They especially feared the seemingly arbitrary discretionary authority that colonial judges had exercised. Indeed, because of the confusion flowing from the different metropolitan and provincial sources of American law, the discretionary authority of colonial judges had often been far greater than that exercised by judges in England itself. The result, as Thomas Jefferson put it in 1776, was that Americans had come to view judicial activity as "the eccentric impulses of whimsical, capricious designing man"; by contrast, said Jefferson, they had come to believe that their legislatures, because they represented the people and had been the guardians of their liberties against royal encroachment, could be trusted to dispense justice "equally and impartially to every description of men." By having the new state legislatures write down the laws in black and white, the Revolutionaries aimed to circumscribe the much-resented former judicial discretion and to turn the judge into what Jefferson hoped would be "a mere machine."[5]

Consequently, nearly all the Revolutionary states to one degree or another attempted to weed out archaic English laws and legal technicalities and to simplify and codify parts of the common law. Society, it was said, often with ample quotations from the Italian legal reformer Cesare Beccaria, needed "but few laws, and these simple, clear, sensible, and easy in their application to the actions of

men." Only through scientific codification and strict judicial observance of "the letter of the law," said William Henry Drayton, a major
political figure of South Carolina, in 1778, quoting Beccaria, could
the people be protected from becoming "slaves to the magistrates."[6]

The Enlightenment promise of codification was never entirely
lost and continued on as part of radical thinking into the nineteenth
century. Already by the 1780s, however, many Revolutionaries
began to realize that precise legislative enactment was not working
out as they had hoped. Many statutes were enacted and many laws
were printed, but rarely in the way reformers like Jefferson and
Madison had expected. Unstable, annually elected, and logrolling
democratic legislatures broke apart plans for comprehensive legal
codes and passed statutes in such confused and piecemeal ways that
the purpose of simplicity and clarity was undermined. "For every
new law . . . ," declared a disgruntled South Carolinian in 1783,
"acts as rubbish, under which we bury the former."[7] This proliferation of statutes meant that judicial discretion, far from diminishing,
became more prevalent than it had been before the Revolution, as
judges tried to navigate their way through the legal mazes.

By the 1780s many Americans concluded that their popular state
assemblies were not only incapable of simplifying and codifying
the law, but they had become the greatest threat to minority rights
and individual liberties and the principal source of injustice in the
society.

Consequently, with democracy running wild, more and more
American leaders began looking to the once-feared judiciary as a
principal means of restraining these rampaging popular legislatures.
The judges became important checks on the excesses of democracy. As early as 1786 William Plummer, a future US senator and
governor of New Hampshire, concluded that the very "existence"
of America's elective governments had come to depend upon the

judiciary: "that is the only body of men who will have an effective check upon a numerous Assembly."[8]

This heightened confidence in the judiciary is doubly remarkable because it flew in the face of much conventional eighteenth-century wisdom. Getting Americans to believe that judges appointed for life were an integral and independent part of their democratic governments—equal in status and authority to the popularly elected executives and legislatures—was no small accomplishment. Such a change in thinking was a measure of how severe the crisis of the 1780s really was and how deep the disillusionment with popular legislative government had become since the idealistic confidence of 1776.

By the 1780s judges in several states were gingerly and ambiguously moving in isolated but important decisions to impose restraints on what the legislatures were enacting as law. They attempted in effect to say to the legislatures, as Judge George Wythe of Virginia did in 1782, "Here is the limit of your authority, and, hither, shall you go, but no further." Yet cautious and tentative as they were, such attempts by the judiciary "to declare the nullity of a law passed in its forms by the legislative power, without exercising the power of that branch," were not readily justified, for they raised, in the words of Judge Edmund Pendleton of Virginia, "a deep, and important, and . . . a tremendous question, the decision of which might involve consequences to which gentlemen may not have extended their ideas."[9]

Even those who agreed that many of the laws passed by the state legislatures in the 1780s were unjust and even unconstitutional, nevertheless could not agree that judges ought to have the authority to declare such legislation void. For judges to declare laws enacted by popularly elected legislatures as unconstitutional and invalid seemed flagrantly inconsistent with free popular government. Such judicial usurpation, said Richard Spraight of North Carolina, was "absurd" and "operated as an absolute negative on the proceedings of the Legislature, which no judiciary ought ever to possess." Instead of being governed by their representatives in the assembly, the people would be subject to the will of a few individuals in the court, "who united in their own persons the legislative and judiciary powers"—a despotism, said Spraight, more insufferable than that of the Roman decemvirate or of any monarchy in Europe.[10]

Most Americans, even those deeply fearful of the legislative abuses of the 1780s, were too fully aware of the modern positivist conception of law—law as legislative will, which meant, as Blackstone had preached in his *Commentaries on the Laws of England*, that whatever the representative legislature enacted, however unjust, was law, to accept easily any kind of judicial review. Moreover, they knew only too well from their colonial experience with arbitrary and uncertain judicial determinations the dangers of allowing the judges too much discretion. All this worked against permitting judges to set aside laws made by the elected representatives of the people. "This," said a perplexed James Madison in 1788, "makes the Judiciary Department paramount in fact to the Legislature, which was never intended and can never be proper."[11]

Yet judicial review of some form did develop in these early decades of the new Republic. What was it? And how did it arise? Given the founders' confused view of judicial review as improper and dangerous or, at best, as an exceptional and awesome political act, simply adding up the several examples during the 1780s and 1790s in which the courts set aside legislative acts as unconstitutional can never explain its origins.

The sources of something as significant and forbidding as judicial review could never lie in the accumulation of a few sporadic judicial precedents, but had to flow from fundamental changes taking place in the Americans' ideas of government and law. As a result of the heavy criticism of their revolutionary actions in the 1770s and 1780s, the legislatures were rapidly losing their exclusive authority as the representatives of the people, and legal sovereignty, even as Blackstone understood it, as the final supreme lawmaking authority, was being located not in any legislative body but in the people at large.

Many Americans were coming to regard the state legislatures as simply another kind of magistracy, and the supposed lawmaking of the legislatures as simply the promulgation of decrees to which the people, standing outside the entire government, had never given their full and unqualified assent.

Therefore, it was possible to argue, as one Rhode Islander did in 1787, that all acts of a legislature were still "liable to examination and scrutiny by the people, that is, by the Supreme Judiciary, their servants for this purpose; and those that militate with the fundamental laws, or impugn the principles of the constitution, are to be judicially set aside as void, and of no effect."[12]

It was left to Alexander Hamilton in *Federalist* No. 78, however, to draw out most fully the logic of this argument. The so-called representatives of the people in the state legislatures, said Hamilton, did not really embody the people, as Parliament, for example, presumably embodied the people of Britain. On the contrary, they were really only one kind of servant of the people with a limited delegated authority to act on their behalf. Americans, said Hamilton, had no intention of allowing "the representatives of the people to substitute their will to that of their constituents." In fact, it was "far more rational to suppose, that the courts were designed to be an intermediate body between the people and the legislature, in order, among other things, to keep the latter within the limits assigned their authority." Judges, Hamilton suggested, were just another kind of servant or agent of the sovereign people.

Therefore, said Hamilton, in summarizing a common emerging view, the authority of the judges to set aside acts of the legislatures lay in the fact that in America real and ultimate sovereignty rested with the people themselves, not with their representatives in the legislatures. Judicial review did not "by any means suppose a superiority of the judicial to the legislative power. It only supposes that the power of the people is superior to both; and that where the will of the legislature declared in its statutes, stands in opposition to that of the people, declared in the constitution, the judges . . . ought to regulate their decisions by the fundamental laws, rather than by those which are not fundamental."[13]

Of course, arguing that judges were equally agents of the people alongside the legislators had unanticipated consequences. If judges were actually agents of the people, then perhaps the people should elect them. And sure enough by 1805, if not before, men were arguing that judges should be elected. Today the people in thirty-nine states in one form or another elect their judges. This development was not anything Hamilton would have wanted.

Establishing the judiciary as a separate and equal agent or servant of the people alongside the legislatures and executives may have been crucial in justifying judicial independence and in granting judges the authority to void legislative acts, but by itself it did not create what came to be called judicial review. The idea of fundamental law and its embodiment in a written constitution were also important.

Almost all eighteenth-century Englishmen on both sides of the Atlantic had recognized something called fundamental law as a guide to the moral rightness and constitutionality of ordinary law and politics. Nearly everyone repeatedly invoked Magna Carta and other fundamental laws of the English constitution. Theorists as different as Locke and Bolingbroke referred equally to the basic principles of the constitution as fundamental law. Even the rise of legislative sovereignty in eighteenth-century England did not displace this prevalent notion of fundamental law. Blackstone himself, despite his commitment to legislative sovereignty, believed that Parliament was limited by what he called an overriding natural law.

Yet all these theoretical references to the principles of the constitution and fundamental law had little day-to-day practical importance. At best this fundamental or natural law of the English constitution was seen as a kind of moral inhibition or conscience existing in the minds of legislators and others. It was so basic and primal, so imposing and political, that it was really enforceable only by the popular elective process or ultimately by the people's right of revolution. Eighteenth-century Englishmen talked about fundamental or natural law, invoked it constantly in their rhetoric, but had great difficulty conceiving of it as something they could call upon in their everyday political and legal business.

The written Revolutionary constitutions of 1776–77, however, gave revolutionary Americans a handle with which to grasp this otherwise insubstantial fundamental law. Suddenly the fundamental law and the first principles that Englishmen had referred to for generations had a degree of explicitness and solid reality that they never before quite had. The constitution in America, said James Iredell of North Carolina in 1787, was thus not "a mere imaginary thing, about which ten thousand different opinions may be formed, but a written document to which all may have recourse, and to which, therefore, the judges cannot witfully blind themselves."[14]

But were the judges to have an exclusive authority to determine what was constitutional and what was not? All Americans agreed that the written constitution, as Edmund Pendleton of Virginia conceded in 1782, "must be considered as a rule obligatory upon every department, not to be departed from on any occasion."[15] It was not immediately evident to Pendleton or to others, however, that the judiciary had any special or unique power to invoke this obligatory rule in order to limit the other departments of the government, particularly the legislatures.

In other words, it was clear by the 1780s that legislatures in America were supposed to be bound by explicitly written constitutions in ways that the English Parliament was not. But it was not yet clear that the courts by themselves were able to enforce those boundaries upon the legislatures. "The great argument is," said James Iredell in 1786 in summarizing the position of those opposed to judicial review, "that the Assembly have not a right to violate the constitution, yet if they in fact do so, the only remedy is, either by a humble petition that the law may be repealed, or a universal resistance of the people. But that in the mean time, their act, whatever it is, is to be obeyed as a law; for the judicial power is not to presume to question the power of an act of Assembly."[16]

Both Jefferson and Madison thought that judges might act as the guardians of popular rights and might resist encroachments on these rights, but they never believed that judges had any special or unique power to interpret the Constitution. In fact, they remained convinced to the end of their lives that all parts of America's governments had the authority to interpret the fundamental law of the constitution—all departments had what Madison called "a *concurrent* right to expound the constitution." When the several departments disagreed in their understanding of the fundamental law, wrote Madison in *Federalist* No. 49, only "an appeal to the people themselves, . . . can alone declare its true meaning, and enforce its observance."[17]

Written constitutions, including the Bill of Rights, remained for Jefferson and Madison a set of great first principles that the several governmental departments, including the judiciary, could appeal to in those extraordinary occasions of violation; but since none of these departments could "pretend to an exclusive or superior right of settling the boundaries between their respective powers," the ultimate appeal in these quasi-revolutionary situations had to be to the people.[18] This was not judicial review as we have come to know it.

In other words, many Revolutionaries or founders still thought that fundamental law, even when expressed in a written constitution, was so fundamental, so different in kind from ordinary law, that its invocation had to be essentially an exceptional and awesomely delicate political exercise. The courts might on occasion set aside legislation that violated fundamental law, but such an act could not be a part of routine judicial business; it necessarily had to be an extraordinary expression of public authority, the kind of extreme and remarkable action the people themselves would take if they could. This kind of judicial review was, as it has been aptly described, simply a "substitute for revolution."[19]

This is why many of the delegates to the Philadelphia Convention in 1787 still regarded judicial nullification of legislation with a sense of awe and wonder, impressed, as Elbridge Gerry was, that "in some States, the Judges had actually set aside laws as being against the Constitution." This is also why many others in the Convention, including James Wilson and George Mason, wanted to join the judges with the executive in a council of revision and thus give the judiciary a double negative over the laws. They considered that the power of the judges by themselves to declare unconstitutional laws void was too extreme, too exceptional, and too fearful an act to be used against all those ordinary unjust, unwise, and dangerous laws that were nevertheless not "so unconstitutional as to justify the Judges in refusing to give them effect."[20]

Such remarks suggest that most of the founders, even when they conceded the power of judges to void unconstitutional legislation in very clear cases, scarcely conceived of such a power in modern terms. They simply could not yet imagine the courts having the authority to expound constitutions in a routine judicial manner. For this reason some congressmen in 1792 debated a regular procedure for federal judges to notify Congress officially whenever they declared a law unconstitutional—so nervous were they over the gravity of such a bold judicial action.[21]

For many Americans then, judicial review remained an extraordinary and solemn political action, akin to the interposition of the states suggested by Jefferson and Madison in the Kentucky and Virginia Resolutions of 1798—something to be invoked only on the rare occasions of flagrant and unequivocal violations of the Constitution. It was not to be exercised in doubtful cases of unconstitutionality and thus could not be an aspect of ordinary judicial activity.

As Justice Samuel Chase said in *Hylton v. the United States* (1796), if the unconstitutionality of Congress's law had been at all "doubtful," he would have been bound "to receive the construction of the legislature." As late as 1800 Justices Bushrod Washington and William Paterson in *Cooper v. Telfair* agreed that judicial review was an extraordinary act to be only rarely exercised. "The presumption," said Washington, ". . . must always be to favour the validity of laws, if the contrary is not clearly demonstrated." For the Supreme Court "to pronounce any law void," said Paterson, there "must be a clear and unequivocal breach of the constitution, not a doubtful and argumentative implication." This had to be the position of judges as long as judicial review seemed to resemble the political momentousness of, say, Jefferson's 1798 idea of state nullification of a federal statute.[22]

The idea of fundamental written law, as important as it was, therefore could not by itself have led to the development of America's judicial review. Other countries since the eighteenth century have had formal rigid and written constitutions—Belgium and France, for example—without allowing their courts on a regular basis to set aside legislative acts that conflict with these written constitutions, not to mention construing these constitutions in order to do justice.

Written constitutions by themselves did not create the peculiarly American process of judicial review in the early Republic. Judicial review, as it came to be practiced in the United States, is so pervasive, so powerful, and so much a part of our everyday judicial proceedings that the presence of a written fundamental law can scarcely explain its development.

It cannot explain it because what gives significance to our conception of a constitution as written fundamental law is not that it is written or that it is fundamental, but rather that it runs in our ordinary court system. America's constitutions may be higher laws, but they are just like all our other lowly laws in that they are discrete, fixed texts created at a historical moment and implemented through the normal ordinary practice of adversarial justice in the regular courts.

Some countries with written constitutions—Brazil, for example—permit their supreme courts to pass on the constitutionality of legislation before it is enacted into law. But exercising super-public or super-judicial authority in this way is not how most American courts operate. Judicial review results from two litigants contesting an issue using routine legal processes in the regular court system. The fact that our written fundamental constitutions, our public laws, are interpreted and construed in a routine fashion in our ordinary court system, and not in some super-public supreme court, is at the heart of our peculiar practice of judicial review.

Thus, the source of judicial review as Americans understand it today lay not in the idea of fundamental law or in written constitutions, but in the transformation of this written fundamental law into the kind of law that could be expounded and construed in the ordinary court system.

We cannot appreciate what opening the Constitution to routine judicial construction really signified unless we understand how important judicial interpretation was to the workings of the common law. The eighteenth-century English constitution was essentially a judge-made constitution. The common law that underlay the constitution remained largely unwritten and was really an accumulation of judicial decisions, precedents, and interpretations that went back centuries. Of course, by the eighteenth century, parliamentary statutes had added considerably to the common law and could and did amend it at will. But the English judges still had to fit these statutes into the whole system of law and to make sense of the written law in particular cases.

Thus, the English common law judges, despite having to bow to the sovereignty of Parliament, were left with an extraordinary amount of room for statutory and common law interpretation and construction for the purpose of doing justice. And, as Blackstone pointed out, there were well worked out rules for judges to follow in construing and interpreting the law—rules that Hamilton in *The Federalist* No. 83 called "rules of common sense, adopted by the courts in the construction of the laws."[23]

Although Edmund Randolph, as a member of the Committee of Detail in the Constitutional Convention, had suggested that "the construction of a constitution . . . necessarily differs from that of a law," turning the Constitution into a law cognizable and constructed by the courts was precisely what was happening.[24] Federalist judges, culminating in the decisions of the Marshall Court, gradually and in piecemeal fashion developed judicial review by collapsing the distinction between fundamental and ordinary law. In their various decisions from the 1780s into the early nineteenth century, they brought the higher law of the several constitutions into the rubric of ordinary law and subjected that higher law to the long-standing common law rules of exposition and construction as if it were no different from a lowly statute.

In effect, judges took all the wide-ranging powers of explication and interpretation that they had traditionally wielded in reconciling ordinary statutes with the common law and applied them to the fundamental law of the constitutions themselves. They even began to bring the new federal Constitution into ordinary courtrooms. American judges began to construe the all-too-brief words of the Constitution in relation to subject matter, intention, context, and reasonableness as if they were the words of an ordinary statute.[25]

The result was the beginning of the creation of a special body of textual exegeses and legal expositions and precedents that have come to be called constitutional law. This accumulative body of constitutional law in America is over two hundred years old, and there is nothing quite like it anywhere else in the world.

This process of equating constitutional and ordinary law has aptly been called "the legalization of fundamental law."[26] It might equally be called the domestication of the Constitution, for it tamed what had hitherto been an object of fearful significance and wonder to the point where it could routinely run in the ordinary court system. Considering the Constitution, in the wise words of legal scholar Gerald Gunther, as "a species of law and accordingly cognizable in courts of law" permitted judges not only to expound and construct the Constitution as if it were an ordinary statute but also to expect regular enforcement of the Constitution as if it were a simple statute.[27]

The momentous implications of this transformation cannot be exaggerated. Because, in Supreme Court Justice John Marshall's words, it was "emphatically the province and duty of the judicial department to say what the law is," treating the Constitution as mere law was immensely important. That law had to be expounded and interpreted and applied to particular cases, which gave special constitutional authority to American judges not shared by most judges throughout the world; it was what made American judicial review possible.[28]

Although this legalization of fundamental law has been attributed to the "deliberate design" of John Marshall, it developed over too many years and became too widely acceptable to be the product of a single person's intentions, however crucially important he may have been. In fact, from the Revolution to the early years of the nineteenth century the transformation occurred in gradual but fitful steps. The initial identification of fundamental law with a written constitution was followed by the need to compare this written constitution with other laws, which required granting the judiciary the role of ultimately determining which law was superior. This in turn led to the blurring of constitutional and ordinary law in the regular court system, which resulted finally in the legal interpretation of fundamental law in accord with what Hamilton, in his 1791 argument justifying the incorporation of the Bank of the United States, called "the usual and established rules of construction" applied to statutory and other ordinary law. All of these halting steps can be traced in the arguments and decisions of the period.

This legalization of fundamental law and the development of judicial review went hand in hand with the demarcation of an exclusive sphere of legal activity for judges. If determining constitutional law were to be simply a routine act of legal interpretation and not an earthshaking political exercise, then the entire process of adjudication had to be removed from politics and from legislative tampering.

After 1800 judges shed their traditional broad and ill-defined political and magisterial roles that had previously identified them with the executive branch and adopted roles that were much more exclusively legal and judicial. Judges withdrew from politics, promoted the development of law as a science known best by trained experts, and limited their activities to the regular courts, which became increasingly professional and less burdened by popular juries. The behavior of Samuel Chase in politically haranguing juries from the bench and the actions of John Jay and Oliver Ellsworth in performing diplomatic missions while sitting as justices of the Supreme Court were not duplicated by subsequent justices. The Supreme Court developed a keener sense of its exclusively judicial character. As early as *Hayburn's Case* in 1792, several justices of the Supreme Court protested against Congress assigning administrative and magisterial duties to them on the grounds that it violated separation of powers.

At the same time as the judges abandoned their earlier magisterial role that in the colonial period had connected them with the chief magistrates—that is, the executives—they began assuming more and more what might be called lawmaking authority for themselves. As the courts pulled back from politics, they attempted to designate some important issues as particular issues of law that were within their exclusive jurisdiction and not within the domain of legislatures. Jurists began to draw lines around what was political or legislative and what was legal or judicial and to justify the distinctions by the doctrine of separation of powers.

As early as 1787 Alexander Hamilton argued in the New York assembly that the state constitution prevented anyone from being deprived of his rights except "by the law of the land" or, as a recent act of the assembly had put it, "by due process of law," which, said Hamilton in an astonishing and novel twist, had "a precise technical import." These words, he contended, were "only applicable to the process and proceedings of the courts of justice; they can never be referred to an act of legislature," even though the legislature had written them.[29]

Judges mistrustful of democracy were eager to downplay the importance of popular lawmaking. "The acts of the legislature form but a small part of that code from which the citizen is to learn his duties, of the magistrate his power and rule of action," declared the presiding judge Moses Levy in the Pennsylvania cordwainers' trial of 1806. These legislative acts were simply the "temporary emanations of a body, the component members of which are subject to perpetual change," and they applied "principally to the political exigencies of the day." Only the unwritten common law could supply what the society legally needed. Only "that invaluable code" composed of ancient precedents and customs could ascertain and define, "with a critical precision, and with a consistency that no fluctuating political body could or can attain, not only the civil rights of property, but the nature of all crimes from treason to trespass." The conclusion was clear. Only the common law whose "rules are the result of the wisdom of ages" could adapt to the novel and shifting circumstances of modernity and regulate "with a sound discretion most of our concerns in civil and social life."[30]

The Federalists of the 1790s were eager to drain political and legal authority away from the popularly elected state legislatures and deposit it the courts, especially the federal courts. They began claiming that the common law of crimes ran in the federal court system; that is, they contended that the federal courts could use something called an American common law—a body of precedents and practices drawn from the unwritten English common law and adapted to American conditions—to punish crimes against the United States and its government, even in the absence of specific federal criminal statutes.

Nothing frightened the opponents of the Federalists, the Jeffersonian Republicans, more than this claim. The common law, the Republicans pointed out, "was a complete system for the management of all the affairs of a country. It . . . went to all things for which laws are necessary." Common law jurisdiction relating to crimes, said Madison, "would confer on the judicial department a discretion little short of legislative power." If the federal courts could use the "vast and multifarious" body of the common law to control American behavior, then, concluded Madison in his famous "Report" of January 1800 to the Virginia Assembly, the courts alone might "new model the whole political fabric of the country."[31]

Although the federal judges denied that they were trying to new-model the political fabric of the country, they did attempt to use the common law to expand national authority in a variety of ways. During the trials of the rebels in the Whiskey and Fries Rebellions, the federal courts used the federal common law to justify the federal government's attempt to bring to trial and punish the rebels' violations of state law and state practices. "Although, in ordinary cases, it would be well to accommodate our practice with that of the state," declared district judge Richard Peters in the trial of the Whiskey rebels, "yet the judiciary of the United States should not be fettered and controlled in its operations, by a strict adherence to state regulations and practice."[32] The federal courts believed that they had an inherent responsibility to defend the national government against those who would subvert its authority.

When some of the Federalists began claiming that the federal courts could use the criminal common law to punish seditious libel even without a sedition act, the Republicans became truly alarmed. The claim that federal judiciary could use the common law to punish crimes, Jefferson declared in 1799, was the "most formidable" doctrine that the Federalists had ever set forth. He told Edmund Randolph that all that the Federalist monocrats and aristocrats had done to tyrannize over the people—creating the Bank, Jay's Treaty, even the Sedition Act of 1798—were "solitary, inconsequential timid things in comparison with the audacious, barefaced and sweeping pretension to a system of law for the US without the adoption of their legislature, and so infinitely beyond their power to adopt."[33] If the Federalists were ever able to establish this doctrine, Jefferson believed that the state courts would be put out of business. As far as he was concerned, there could be no law apart from the popular will of the nation. Since that will had never established the common law for the United States, and indeed had no right to do so anyway for such a limited government, the federal government contained no such common law.[34]

In 1800 when the Jeffersonian Republicans came to power, they were angry enough at the Supreme Court that they would have reduced it to a nullity if they could have. They came close. They abolished the Judiciary Act of 1801 by which the Federalists had created a appellate system of circuit courts with sixteen new federal judges and they sought to use impeachment as means of judicial removal.

In that heightened political climate the newly appointed chief justice, John Marshall, sought to avoid the most explosive and partisan issues of the 1790s. He used his court to retreat from the advanced and exposed political positions that the Federalists had tried to stake out for the federal judiciary, including the enlarged definitions of treason and the claim that the common law of crimes ran in the federal courts.

In 1803 in a marvelously indirect assertion of the Supreme Court's authority to declare an act of Congress unconstitutional, Marshall, in the case of *Marbury v. Madison*, eased some of the partisan tensions. Many Federalists wanted Marshall to declare the Republicans' repeal of the Judiciary Act of 1801 unconstitutional, for it had removed sixteen judges in blatant violation of the Constitution's guarantee of life tenure. But Marshall knew that if the Court did that, its decision would be ignored, and the authority of the Court would be diminished. Instead, he used the *Marbury* decision to declare that Section 13 of the Judiciary Act of 1789 granting the Supreme Court the power to issue judicial commands or mandamuses was unconstitutional—thus limiting he authority of his own Court.

This shrewdly circuitous and narrow decision avoided all the serious political repercussions that would have occurred if the Court had taken on the Republicans' repeal of the Judiciary Act of 1801. Although Marshall's decision in *Marbury v. Madison* has since taken on immense historical significance as the first assertion by the Supreme Court of its right to declare acts of Congress unconstitutional, few in 1803 saw its far-reaching implications. Certainly, it didn't trouble most Republicans. If Marshall wanted to circumscribe the power of the Supreme Court, as he did in the *Marbury* decision, then he had every right to do so. But, said Jefferson, the judiciary was not the only branch of the government that had the right to interpret the Constitution. The executive and legislature could too. To grant the courts the exclusive authority to decide what laws were constitutional, declared Jefferson in 1804, "would make the judiciary a despotic branch."[35] Since Marshall had not explicitly claimed that the Supreme Court was the only part of the government with the right and duty to interpret the Constitution, his assertion of judicial authority in the *Marbury* decision was limited and ambiguous. In fact, it was the only time in Marshall's long tenure as chief justice in which the Supreme Court declared an act of Congress unconstitutional.

The *Marbury* decision had implications that went beyond an assertion of judicial review. Although Marshall may have seemed to have reduced the power of the Court, at the same time he carved out an exclusive role for it that was in line with what judges since the 1780s had been developing. "Some questions were political," said Marshall; "they respect the nation, not individual rights" and thus were "only politically examinable." But questions involving the vested rights of individuals were different; they were in their "nature, judicial, and must be tried by the judicial authority."[36]

Placing legal boundaries around issues such as property rights and contracts had the effect of isolating these issues from popular tampering, partisan debate, and the clashes of interest group politics. The power to interpret constitutions became a matter not of political interest to be determined by legislatures but a matter of the "fixed principles" of a domesticated constitutional law to be determined only by judges.

Without the protection of the courts and the intricacies of the common law, Alexander Dallas, Supreme Court reporter and later Madison's secretary of the Treasury, drew out the significance of the distinction Marshall and other judges had made between the public and private realms. In his address composed in 1805 in the midst of an intense debate in Pennsylvania over the role of the judiciary, Dallas contended that without the protection of the courts and the mysterious intricacies of the common law, "rights would remain forever without remedies and wrongs without redress." The people of Pennsylvania, the address declared, could no longer count on their popularly elected legislature to solve many of the problems of their lives. "For the varying exigencies of social life, for the complicated interests of an enterprising nation, the positive acts of the legislature can provide little fundamental protection alone."[37]

It is hard to imagine a more severe indictment of popular democracy. Many apparently had come to believe that a society as unruly and as democratic as America's needed the moderating influence of an aristocracy, an aristocracy that was free of marketplace interests. Outside of the South, however, aristocracy in America was hard to come by. But necessity invented one. In *Federalist* No. 35, Alexander Hamilton had argued passionately that, unlike merchants, mechanics, and farmers, "the learned professions," by which he meant mainly lawyers, "truly form no distinct interest in society." They could therefore play the same role of disinterested political leadership that the landed aristocracy in England played. They "will feel a neutrality to the rivalships between the different branches of industry" and will be most likely to be "an impartial arbiter" between the diverse interests of the society.[38]

That, it seemed, was what happened. When the Frenchman Alexis de Tocqueville visited America in the 1830s, he pointed out that lawyers had come to constitute whatever aristocracy America possessed, at least in the North. Through their influence on the judiciary, they tempered America's turbulent and unruly majoritarian governments and promoted the rights of individuals and minorities. "The courts of justice," Tocqueville said, "are the visible organs by which the legal profession is enabled to control the democracy."[39] It is still a shrewd judgment.

Chapter 7

The Great Demarcation
Between Public and Private

In his *Marbury* decision Chief Justice Marshall drew a distinction between political matters that were the preserve of political bodies on the one hand and judicial matters that were the exclusive province of the courts on the other. In making this distinction Marshall was in effect recognizing two separate realms, a public one and private one. Distinguishing between public and private spheres, not just in law but also in other areas of life, was an important consequence of the Revolution. In fact, that separation constituted a "great demarcation" between public and private that differentiated the old society of the eighteenth century from the new society of the nineteenth century. For the Western world in general, the sharpening of the difference between private and public marked the transition to modernity.[1]

The fairly clear-cut distinctions between public and private that are taken for granted today did not exist in the American colonial world. Most colonists, for example, could not yet conceive of religion as an entirely private matter beyond the reach of government. Nearly all the eighteenth-century colonies still regarded religion as a public or communal responsibility, and in almost every colony the government maintained at least a semblance of state control or support with public funds. Even in the two colonies of Rhode Island and Pennsylvania that had no official religious establishments, people expected the government to regulate moral discipline, punish blasphemy, and enforce the Sabbath.

Everywhere in the colonies governments relied on the enlisting and mobilization of the power of private persons to carry out public ends. If the eighteenth-century city of New York wanted its streets cleaned or paved, for example, it did not hire contractors or create a "public works" department; instead it issued ordinances obliging each person in the city to clean or repair the street abutting his house or shop.[2]

Most public action—from the establishing of religion and the creation of colleges to the building of wharfs and the maintaining of roads—depended upon private energy and private funds. Eighteenth-century governments had very few financial resources; what they did have was legal authority, and they exploited that legal authority in order to get things done without incurring any direct public costs. They even required criminal defendants who were acquitted to pay the costs of their trials. They offered corporate charters, licenses, franchises, and various other legal immunities in order to entice private persons to carry out public responsibilities that the governments themselves lacked the funds to do.

All this suggests that eighteenth-century colonial society and culture still retained premodern elements that have since been lost. In the colonial ancien régime the modern distinctions between state and society, public and private, were not at all clear. The king's inherited rights to govern the realm—his prerogatives—were as much private as they were public, just as the people's ancient rights or liberties were as much public as they were private. Public institutions had private rights and private persons had public obligations. The king's prerogatives or his premier rights to govern the realm grew out of his private position as the wealthiest of the wealthy and the largest landowner in the society; his government had really begun as an extension of his royal household. But in a like manner, all private households or families—"those small subdivisions of Government," one colonist called them—had public responsibilities to help the king govern.[3]

The colonial governments carried out their responsibilities without the aid of elaborate bureaucracies; they relied instead on the private society. On the eve of the Revolution all the expenses of the government of South Carolina came to less than £8000 a year. Colonial Massachusetts had a society of three hundred thousand people, yet it spent less than £25,000 a year on its government, which employed only six "full-time officials" and less than a thousand "part-time officials." Even this notion of "full-time" and "part-time" officials is anachronistic and misleading, for no one yet conceived of a permanent civil service in the local colonial governments or of political officeholding as a paid profession. It is true that members of the Massachusetts assembly were paid for their services, but this practice was unusual, and it horrified many observers. Most officeholding, as William Douglass, a Scottish immigrant-physician, observed, was viewed, with varying degrees of plausibility, as a public obligation that private persons *"serving gratis or generously"* owed to the community.[4]

Only in the context of these traditional assumptions about the blurring of state and society can we appreciate the private nature of officeholding in the colonies. Since everyone in the society had an obligation to help govern the realm commensurate with his social rank—the king's being the greatest because he stood at the top of the social hierarchy—important offices were supposed to be held only by those who were already worthy and had already achieved economic and social superiority. Just as gentlemen were expected to staff the officers' corps of the army, so were independent gentlemen of leisure and education expected to supply leadership for government. Nearly all the colonial leaders felt the weight of this claim upon them and often agonized and complained about it. "Public offices," said Jefferson, "are, what they should be, burthens to those appointed to them, which it would be wrong to decline, though foreseen to bring with them intense labor, and great private loss."[5]

Thomas Hutchinson, the most hated loyalist in America, never regarded his many offices as anything but public obligations placed upon him by his distinguished and wealthy position in Massachusetts society. "I never sought or solicited any posts," he said in 1765; and he insisted that he would willingly give up all claim to honors and emoluments if it would serve the peace of his country.[6] Presumably Hutchinson never lost money from his officeholding—his confiscated estate as a loyalist was worth £98,000—but most local officeholders, from grand jurors to justices of the peace, did serve without salary. In some communities governments often had trouble getting people to take on certain offices. Of course, many offices offered the holders incentives in the form of fees, rewards, or benefits, sometimes quite lucrative ones. But always it was assumed that granting such offices together with their perquisites was the best way for these premodern governments to get things done without incurring any direct public costs.

Since the society and state were supposed to be identical, government offices seemed to belong to men of high social rank in the same way that the throne belonged to the king. Indeed, many officeholders tended to regard their offices as a virtual species of private property that they could pass on to members of their families. Seats on Virginia grand juries were perpetuated within families almost as frequently as seats on the vestries and county courts. In

Cambridge, Massachusetts, between 1700 and 1780 three successive Andrew Boardmans not only served almost continuously as town clerk and town treasurer but were also elected for ninety-three terms as selectman, representative, and moderator.[7]

During the half-century before the Revolution, more than 70 percent of the representatives elected to the New Jersey assembly were related to previously elected legislators. The situation in South Carolina was similar. Dominant families everywhere monopolized political offices and passed them among themselves, even through successive generations.[8] Although these offices were not quite the seigneuries of ancien régime France, the holders of these public offices did regard them as essentially their private property.

Whether it was the town clerkship in Norwich, Connecticut, or the clerk of the court in Lancaster County, Virginia, in each case a single family held the office for forty or so years before the Revolution. Everywhere in the colonies men resigned offices in favor of their sons and then exulted, as Joseph Read of Pennsylvania did to Edward Shippen III in 1774: "Is it not agreeable to find our Descendants thus honoured?" The practice of "a father resigning his place to his son" was common enough that even Thomas Hutchinson complained that it was "tending to make all offices hereditary."[9]

John Adams knew of what he was speaking when he stressed the importance of family dynasties in New England politics. "Go into every village in New England," he said, "and you will find that the office of justice of the peace, and even the place of representative, which has ever depended only on the freest election of the people, have generally descended from generation to generation, in three or four families at most."[10]

Just as colonial public buildings were no more than elaborate private residences, so too was public business often mingled with private affairs. Merchants used public money for private purposes, and vice versa. Soldiers sued their captains for their back pay. Magistrates lived off the fees and fines they levied. And governors sometimes drew on their personal accounts to raise money to supply troops. That the North Carolina governor even offered in 1765 to pay that portion of the stamp tax pertaining to official documents out of his own pocket indicates just how strange and foreign that eighteenth-century past really is.

Translating the personal, social, and economic power of the leading gentry into political authority was essentially what eighteenth-century politics was about. The process was self-intensifying: social power created political authority, which in turn created more social influence. Some members of the gentry, such as the wealthy landholders of the Connecticut River valley, had enough influence to overawe entire communities. Connecticut River valley gentry like Israel Williams and John Worthington, so imposing as to be called "river gods," used their private social power to become at one time or another selectmen of their towns, representatives to the Massachusetts General Court, members of the Council, provincial court judges, justices of the peace, and colonels of their county regiments. It became impossible to tell where the circle of their authority began: the political authority to grant licenses for taverns or mills, to determine the location of roads and bridges, or to enlist men for military service was of a piece with their wealth and social influence.

This personal structure of eighteenth-century politics, the prevalence of numerous vertical lines of influence converging on particular people of wealth and power, was what made colonial politics essentially a contest among prominent families for the control of state authority. This personal structure of politics, and not simply the age's abhorrence of division, explains the absence of organized political parties in the eighteenth century. Political factions existed, but these were little more than congeries of the leading gentry's personal and family "interests." And it was this personal structure of politics—not any elaborate legal restrictions on the suffrage—that kept most common people from participating in politics.

Although the contending gentry increasingly appealed to the "people" in electoral contests—so much so, as Governor William Shirley of Massachusetts observed in 1742, that the aroused people had "it in their power upon an extraordinary Emergency to double and almost treble their numbers" in elections—much of the time most ordinary folk were not deeply involved in provincial or imperial politics. Sometimes as many as one third of the towns of Massachusetts failed to send representatives to the provincial legislature. At other times gentlemen of influence overawed the electorate and kept it quiet. In a 1758 election in Newport, Rhode Island, noted Ezra Stiles, two hundred out of six hundred eligible freemen did not vote; "one third lie still," he said, "silenced by Connexions."[11]

Because officeholders tended to think of their offices as belonging to them as their private property, they often treated government business as if it were their private business. They conducted official public affairs in secrecy, behind closed doors, and exhibited no awareness that the people-out-doors ought to know what was going behind those closed doors. Before 1765 there was very little discussion of politics in the colonial press. There was certainly none of what today we call "transparency" in governing. Even the activities of the colonial assemblies that were supposed to be representative of the people remained unknown to voters and the people-at-large. No legislative debates were published, and even the votes of the popular representatives went unrecorded. It was as if the government was a private matter involving only those who owned and ran it.

Because office was an extension into government of the private person, the greater the private person, the greater the office. Access to government therefore often came quickly and easily to those who had the necessary social credentials. Thus wealthy John Dickinson was elected to the Delaware assembly in 1760 at the age of twenty-eight and promptly was made its speaker. Social position was more important than age and experience. This was why Daniel Dulany of Maryland, precisely because he inherited great wealth and social position, was able to take over in 1753 the political offices that his father had spent decades in achieving. In a like manner Jonathan Trumbull, a poor, obscure country merchant, was catapulted into speakership of the Connecticut assembly at age twenty-eight and into the council at age twenty-nine simply by his marriage into the ancient and prestigious Robinson family—a connection that gave him, as the Anglican clergyman and historian of colonial Connecticut, Samuel Peters, put it, "the prospect of preferment in civil life."[12]

Everywhere in the colonies those who had sufficient property and social power to exert influence in any way—whether by lending money, doing favors, or supplying employment—created obligations and dependencies that could be turned into political authority. Probably no one in late eighteenth-century America used his property and social position to create political dependencies and political influence more shamelessly than John Hancock. Hancock patronized everyone. He made work for people. He erected homes that he did not need. He built ships that he sold at a loss. He sponsored any and every young man who importuned him. He opened trade shops and staffed them. He purchased a concert hall for public use. He entertained lavishly and habitually treated the Boston populace to wine. John Adams recalled that "not less than a thousand families were, every day in the year, dependent on Mr. Hancock for their daily bread." He went through the mercantile fortune he had inherited from his uncle, but he formed one of the most elaborate networks of political dependency in eighteenth-century America and became the single most popular and powerful figure in Massachusetts politics during the last quarter of the century.[13]

But Hancock's private ownership of public power was nothing compared to that of the great slaveholding planters of Virginia. The Virginia planters' private patronage power was enormous, and it enabled them to dominate their local communities and to maintain law and order without the aid of police forces in a manner unmatched in any other colony. They were the protectors, creditors, and counselors of the lesser yeoman farmers in their neighborhood. They lent them money, found jobs or minor posts for their sons, stood as godfathers for their children, handed down clothing to their families, doctored them, and generally felt responsible for the welfare of "our neighbors who depended upon us." During a particularly bad "ague and fever Season" in 1771, "the whole neighbourhood," Landon Carter proudly noted in his diary, "are almost every day sending to me. I serve them all." These Virginia planters were also the vestrymen of their parishes and the lay leaders of the Anglican church, so that the sacredness of religion and the patronage of poor relief further enhanced their authority.[14]

Since the colonial governments lacked most of the coercive powers of a modern state—a few constables and sheriffs scarcely constituted a police force—officeholders relied on their own social respectability and private influence to compel the obedience of ordinary people. Common people could become hog reeves or occupy other lowly offices, but they had no business exercising high political office, since, in addition to being involved in their petty workaday interests, they had no power, no connections, and no social capacity for commanding public allegiance and deference. Thus when in 1759 the governor of Massachusetts appointed as a justice of the peace in Hampshire County someone whose company the other local justices declared they were "never inclined to keep," eleven of the justices resigned in protest, saying that such an appointment would make the office contemptible in the eyes of the people and diminish their ability to enforce the law. So too did South Carolinians in 1761 condemn a crown-appointed placeman as chief justice of the colony on the grounds that he was an "Irishman of the lowest class," ignorant of the law, and socially "contemptible." For mechanics and other manual laborers, holding high office was virtually impossible while they remained in their inferior status and were engaged in their selfish market interests.[15]

It was crucially important in this old society that public officials, including military officers, possess the proper private social credentials. In 1757 Governor Robert Dinwiddie of Virginia severely dressed down an underling who had shown little or no awareness of this requirement. Dinwiddie's subordinate had conferred a colonelcy on a man who "has no Estate in the County, and keeps an Ordinary," and bestowed a captaincy on "a Person insolvent and not able to pay his Levy." This was outrageous, said Dinwiddie, because no one of importance will associate with "such Persons that have neither Land nor Negroes."[16]

Shrewd artisans and petty traders who had wealth and grand political ambitions, such as Roger Sherman of Connecticut, knew they needed to retire from business and become gentlemen if they were to acquire high public office. Benjamin Franklin was especially scrupulous on this point—perhaps because his sights were higher and his enemies more numerous. Franklin timed his entrance into public officeholding only when in 1747 he had firmly established his private status as a wealthy gentleman. To commemorate his coming out into gentility he even commissioned Robert Feke to paint a mannered and foppish portrait to honor the occasion. Later in his life, however, when the identification between the social hierarchy and public officeholding had broken down and he had become a wigless republican hero, Franklin conveniently forgot about this monarchical portrait.[17]

The stability of the political system depended on the social authority of the political leaders being visible and incontestable, which was why governments were often eager and anxious to confer social honors and titles on their officers. Justices of the peace were invariably "Esq."; assemblymen and many selectmen were "Mr." In fact, wrote the English jurist William Blackstone, "honours and offices are in their nature convertible and synonymous." Social distinctions, including titles, were the prerequisites of high government office: "that the people may know and distinguish such as are set over them, in order to yield them their due respect and obedience."[18]

No wonder that officials were so sensitive to public criticism of their private character. They knew only too well—"these are dry commonplace observations, known to everyone"—that their ability to govern rested on their personal reputations. In fact, as the future loyalist Jonathan Sewell put it in 1766, "the person and the office are so connected in the minds of greatest part of mankind, that a contempt of the former, and a veneration for the latter are totally incompatible." It seemed imperative to many that only men of the highest social status should hold public office.[19]

This identification between social and political authority, private and public leadership, ran deep in this traditional monarchical world. No presumption about politics was in fact more basic to this old society and separated it more from the emerging democratic world of the nineteenth century.

The Revolution changed everything. Public and private spheres, state and society, became separated, and public officeholding lost much of its connection to the private world; indeed, the separation between social and political superiority, which the old society had sometimes desperately sought to bring together, became a measure of democracy. Politics became more transparent, more open to ordinary people, and governments began doing things by themselves instead of enlisting private wealth and resources for public purposes.

Unlike revolutionary France, the American Revolution had no one crucial moment, no night like August 4, 1789, in which the revolutionaries suddenly did away with feudal-like traditions that had existed for centuries. In the United States what had to be changed was different, less formidable, less legally entrenched, and the changes took place more slowly, more piecemeal, more confusedly. It was not easy to separate private life from public power, and the presumption that the officeholder somehow owned the office lingered on. For this reason, when John Adams succeeded Washington as president in 1797, he felt he could not replace members of his predecessors' cabinet. So too when Jefferson became president in 1801, he quickly discovered that he couldn't take for granted his power to remove Federalist officeholders, who continued to believe that somehow their offices still belonged to them. The great demarcation was slow but nonetheless relentless.[20]

The goal of the American Revolutionaries was to create republican governments that would abolish the abuses of patronage and patrimonial power that had plagued the old society. In place of dependent subjects they would create republican citizens who were equal and independent and free from dependency on grandees and patrons. But the republican revolution aimed to do more: it sought to assert the primacy of the public good over all private interests, indeed, to separate sharply the public from the private and to prevent the intrusion of private interests into the public realm. These goals compelled Revolutionary Americans to conceive of state power in radically new ways.

Modern conceptions of public power replaced the older archaic ideas of personal monarchical government. No longer could government be viewed as the king's private authority or as a bundle of prerogative rights. Rulers suddenly lost their traditional personal rights to rule, and personal allegiance as a civic bond became meaningless. All the earlier talk of paternal or maternal government, filial allegiance, and mutual contractual obligations between rulers and ruled fell away. With the Revolution the familial image of government under which the colonists had conducted the imperial debate lost all its previous relevance, and the state in America emerged as something very different from what it had been.

The Revolutionary state constitutions eliminated the Crown's prerogatives outright or regranted them to the state legislatures. Overnight the state assemblies became sovereign embodiments of the people, with responsibility for exercising an autonomous public authority, creating a new role for them. Their colonial predecessors had rarely legislated in any modern sense; they had done little more than respond to numerous private petitions and local grievances of individuals and groups. But the Revolution, with its need for revenue, men, and material to wage war, changed all that. The enhanced authority they had been granted by their constitutions, together with the expanded notion of consent underlying all government, gave the state legislatures a degree of public power that the colonial assemblies had never claimed or even imagined. In republican America government would no longer be merely private property and private interests writ large, as it had been in the colonial period. Public and private spheres that earlier had been blended were now separated. The new republican states saw themselves promoting a unitary public interest that was to be clearly distinguishable from the many private interests of their societies. This was America's great demarcation.

Flush with their newly enhanced public power, the republican state governments sought to assert it in direct and unprecedented ways—doing for themselves what they had earlier commissioned private persons to do. They carved out exclusively public spheres of action and responsibility where none had existed before. They drew up plans for improving everything from trade and commerce to roads and waterworks and helped to create a science of political economy for Americans. And they formed their own public organizations with paid professional staffs supported by tax money, not private labor. For many Americans the Revolution had made the "self-management of self-concerns ... the vital part of government."[21]

The city of New York, for example, working under the authority of the state legislature, set up its own public works force to clean its streets and wharves instead of relying on the private residents to do these tasks. By the early nineteenth century the city had become a public institution financed primarily by public taxation and concerned with particularly public concerns. It acquired what it had not had before—the power of eminent domain—and the authority to make decisions without worrying about "whose property is benefited ... or is not benefited." The power of the state to take private property seemed virtually unlimited—as long as the property was taken for exclusively public purposes.[22]

The new republican state governments became more responsive and more accessible to the people. Even before the Declaration of Independence the legislatures began opening up to the people. In 1766 the Massachusetts House of Representatives erected a public gallery for the witnessing of its debates, an important step in the democratization of American political culture. The Pennsylvania assembly followed (somewhat reluctantly) in 1770, and eventually the other legislatures began to reach out to a wider public. From 1765 on, newspapers and pamphlets expanded exponentially.[23]

People began to be interested in what went on in their representative assembles, and they severely criticized the Constitutional Convention of 1787 for its secrecy.

The Revolutionaries aimed to end the practice of families seeming to own the offices of government as a kind of private property and passing them down, as Charles Carroll complained, "like a precious jewel . . . down from *father* to *son*."[24] They declared, in the words of the New Hampshire constitution, that "no office or place whatsoever in government, shall be hereditary—the abilities and integrity requisite in all, not being transmissible to posterity or relations." George Mason in his declaration of rights for the Virginia constitution of 1776 was equally emphatic. "No Man, or Set of Men," he wrote, "are entitled to exclusive or separate Emoluments or Privileges from the Community, but in Consideration of public Services; which not being descendible, or hereditary, the Ideal of a Man born a Magistrate, a Legislator, or a Judge is unnatural and absurd."[25]

To break the hold that private families had on public offices, all states moved to abolish the legal devices of primogeniture and entail where they existed, either by statute or by writing the abolition into their constitutions. These legal devices, as the North Carolina statute of 1784 stated, had tended "only to raise the wealth and importance of particular families and individuals, giving them an unequal and undue influence in a republic, and prove in manifold instances the source of great contention and injustice." Their abolition would therefore "tend to promote that equality of property which is of the spirit and principle of a genuine republic."[26]

The Revolution thus made a major change in the older patterns of inheritance. Although some states continued the traditional practice of favoring the eldest son, most of the new inheritance laws broke with a patrilineal definition of kinship and recognized the

equal rights of daughters and widows in the inheriting and possession of property. In a variety of ways the new state laws not only
abolished the remaining feudal forms of land tenure and enhanced
the commercial nature of real estate, but they also confirmed the
new enlightened republican attitudes toward the family.

Although wives continued to remain dependent on their
husbands, they did gain greater autonomy and some legal recogni-
tion of their rights to hold property separately, to divorce, and to
make contracts and do business in the absence of their husbands.
In the colonial period only New Englanders had recognized the absolute right to divorce, but after the Revolution all the states except
South Carolina developed new liberal laws on divorce.

Even the traditional public emphasis on the meaning of property became privatized. In the old society of the colonial period,
when people talked about property in public—such as property
qualifications for the suffrage or for officeholding—they meant proprietary property. That kind of public property was part of people's
identity and the source of their authority. Such proprietary property
was not the private product of one's labor or a privately owned commercial asset but rather a public means of maintaining one's political independence. Landed property was the most important such
guarantee of autonomy because it was the least transitory, the most
permanent form of property. But southern planters sometimes had
thought of their slaves in these proprietary terms. Recall Governor
Dinwiddie's reference to a man lacking quality because he possessed
"neither Land nor Negroes."[27]

In the decades following the Revolution property became
more and more defined as something personally owned, as a material commodity to be bought and sold in the marketplace. Once
people thought of property in this modern manner, it shed much
of its older sanctified classical meaning as a basis for public identity,

independence, and dominion and became a mere private material possession, having no significance for the running of the state. It was evanescent—"continually changing like the waves of the sea," said Justice Joseph Story, and "a source of comfort of every kind" that belonged to everyone. That kind of modern property, "compared to our other rights, is insignificant and trifling." Such a fleeting, trifling kind of private property could no longer be the source of independence of a few "opulent and munificent citizens"; instead it was "only one of the incidental rights of the person who possesses it," personally important, no doubt, but scarcely capable of qualifying someone to vote or to participate in government. Under these circumstances, property qualifications for the franchise or officeholding naturally fell away.[28]

With the expansion of the suffrage and the emergence of two competitive political parties—the Federalists and the Jeffersonian Republicans—the turnout of voters exploded in both state and federal elections. Participation grew from 20 percent in the 1790s to 80 percent or more of qualified voters in the first decade of the nineteenth century. Anti-elitism flourished amidst endless appeals to equality, which became the most powerful ideological force in American history. Men without any social standing whatsoever, without any great wealth or other sources of independence, at least in the North, were getting into the offices of government, which now paid salaries. Some of these new men even bragged about their lack of social credentials and claimed that education and wealth should bar men from serving in government. When opponents mocked Simon Snyder, campaigning for governor of Pennsylvania in 1808, as a "clodhopper," he turned the epithet into a badge of honor and used it successfully to win office. Other public figures came to realize that even when they possessed superior private social credentials, it was wise to hide them. Daniel Tomkins, a wealthy attorney and graduate of Columbia College, thought it best in his campaign for governor of New York in 1807 to portray himself as a simple "Farmer's Boy," in contrast to his opponent who was related to the aristocratic Livingston family.

These democratic developments undermined the presumption of the older society that private social credentials ought to determine public authority. Indeed, popular politicians were reversing the older presumption: some of them began using their public offices to acquire wealth and social position. And they weren't embarrassed about it. Congressman Matthew Lyon from Vermont, an Irish immigrant who came to America as a bonded servant, saw nothing wrong with using his office to get government contracts for himself. What difference did it make, he asked on the floor of the House in 1805, if a congressman served "the public for the same reward the public gives another"? Although a member of the House of Representatives, he was also a businessman looking "for customers with whom I can make advantageous bargains to both parties. It is all the same to me whether I contract with an individual or the public." Lyon became one of the wealthiest businessmen in the state of Vermont, if not all of New England.[29]

Thus public and private were changing and coming apart everywhere in the early Republic, but perhaps nowhere more conspicuously than with corporate charters. These legal devices were perfect examples of the way the old society had harnessed private energy and resources for public ends. Dating back to the sixteenth century in England, corporate charters were monopolistic grants of legal privileges and immunities given by the state to private persons and associations to carry out a wide variety of endeavors that were presumably beneficial to the whole society. The East India Company, given a charter by Queen Elizabeth in 1600, was the most famous of the early corporations. In 1606 the English Crown had given such a charter of incorporation to the Virginia Company to settle parts of North America. These corporate privileges were not frequently granted or widely available, and they were made at the initiative of the government, not private interests. Like so much in the ancien régime the corporate charters had recognized no sharp division between public and private. Although the Virginia Company had been composed of private entrepreneurs seeking profits, it was as much public as it was private. The same was true of the corporate charters of Massachusetts Bay (1628), Connecticut (1662), and Rhode Island (1663), as well as those of Harvard, Yale, Princeton, and all the other colleges chartered in the colonial period; these colleges were regarded as public institutions with communal responsibilities, and as such they received tax money and public support.

With the Revolution and its emphasis on the republican res publica or public matters, most state constitution-makers were naturally hostile to the traditional practice of issuing exclusive corporate privileges and licenses to private persons. In a republic, it was said, no person should be allowed to exploit the public's authority for private gain. Thus, several of the states wrote into their revolutionary constitutions declarations that stated, as the North Carolina constitution of 1776 did, that "perpetuities and monopolies are contrary to the genius of a State, and ought not to be allowed."[30]

Consequently, with the Revolution the issue of states granting exclusive monopolistic charters to colleges and businesses aroused strenuous opposition and heated debate. Critics charged that such privileged grants, even when their public purpose seemed obvious, such as those for the College of Philadelphia or the Bank of North America, were repugnant to the spirit of American republicanism, "which does not admit of granting peculiar privileges to any body of men." Such franchises and privileged grants may have made sense in monarchies as devices serving "to circumscribe and limit absolute power." But once the people ruled, these grants of corporate favors seemed pernicious. As Justice John Hobart of New York declared, "all incorporations imply a privilege given to one order of citizens which others do not enjoy, and are so far destructive of the principle of equal liberty which should subsist in every community."[31]

Attempts by the state legislatures to confiscate several corporate charters or to prevent their renewal provoked fiery opposition from the holders of the corporate privileges. The proprietors of the corporations argued that their charters were a species of private property, a vested right, that once granted by the legislature were immune from subsequent legislative tampering. If the state could take this kind of property away, then, they warned, it could take anyone's property away. Defenders of state legislative sovereignty were angered and bewildered by these arguments. Surely, they said, what the state granted in the public interest could be taken back or changed if the public interest wasn't being fulfilled.

The nature of these corporation remained confused. Were they public? Were they private? Could the legislatures tamper with them once they were granted? Were they vested rights beyond government control?

In 1804 the Supreme Court under Chief Justice John Marshall grappled with the issue of a corporation for the first time. In the case of *Head & Amory v. Providence Insurance Company* the Marshall Court accepted the traditional view of a corporation: that it was a public entity with a public charter that by implication could be altered by the legislature that granted it. The decision presumably covered all charters issued for public purposes, including towns, turnpikes, canals, banks, and colleges.[32]

But during the subsequent decade the Court shifted its thinking—as revealed in the case of *Terrett v. Taylor* (1815). In this decision, written by Justice Joseph Story, the Supreme Court separated corporations into two kinds, public and private, s distinction that was new to American law, but in line with the great demarcation that was emerging in the culture. Charters of public corporations that had public purposes might be modified by legislatures under proper limitations; but, said Story, such public corporations included only "counties, towns, and cities." The charters of all other corporations, including businesses and colleges, Story claimed, were species of private property and were protected by the principles of natural justice and the fundamental law of the Constitution.[33]

This set the stage for the Dartmouth College case of 1819. In his creative decision Marshall contended that Dartmouth College was a "private" corporation as defined by Story in *Terrett v. Taylor.* But he then went beyond Story's rather ambiguous reference to the Constitution to find an actual text in the document to protect the corporation from state interference. He declared that the College's charter was a contract under Article I, Section 10, of the United States Constitution—a remarkable claim not easily justified, which is why Marshall said that "It can require no argument to prove, that the circumstances of this case constitute a contract." The decision placed all private corporations—not just colleges, but banks, manufacturing firms, bridges, turnpikes, and other profitable businesses—under the protection of the specific text of the Constitution—contracts that the states could not violate or impair.[34]

The decision infuriated Jefferson. The notion that a corporate charter granted by the legislature became private property untouchable by subsequent legislatures was absurd and violated everything he believed in. Such a doctrine, inculcated by "our lawyers and priests," supposed "that preceding generations held the earth more freely than we do; had a right to impose laws on us, unalterable by ourselves, and that we, in like manner, can make laws and impose burdens on future generations, which they will have no right to alter; in fine, that the earth belongs to the dead and not the living."[35]

If that had been the only development of the corporation, that is, that once granted the corporation became a private vested right or contract that was beyond future legislative tampering, it would have created an intolerable situation. How could a republican government tolerate a favored few receiving monopolistic privileges that could not subsequently be tampered with or revoked? The states evaded this intolerable situation by eventually granting corporate charters to everyone who wanted one, thus turning what had once been an exclusive privilege into a right available to all.

With a huge proportion of the representatives in the state legislatures turning over annually, each special interest in society began clamoring for its own cluster of legal privileges. In the older colonial society, the likely recipients of these corporate charters had been limited in number and more or less socially and politically visible; but in the new egalitarian republics the prospective beneficiaries of these legal privileges were no longer so obvious. As soon as the Massachusetts legislature, for example, granted a bank charter to some Boston entrepreneurs, another group petitioned for a second bank charter, which diluted the monopolistic character of the first charter. Then groups in Newburyport and Worcester sought bank charters, and so on. Thus the corporate charters multiplied in ever increasing numbers.

With this proliferation of corporate grants not only was the traditional exclusivity of the corporate charter undermined, but also the public power of the state governments was dispersed and scattered. As early as 1802 James Sullivan, Massachusetts attorney general, warned that "the creation of a great variety of corporate interests . . . must have a direct tendency to weaken the powers of government." But Massachusetts continued to dole out these pieces of public power into private hands in a profligate manner to the point, as a Massachusetts governor put it, that there was a danger that the state might end up with "only the very shadow of sovereignty."[36]

The legislatures incorporated not just colleges and banks but insurance companies and manufacturing concerns, and they licensed entrepreneurs to operate bridges, roads, and canals. The states issued eleven charters of incorporation between 1781 and 1785, twenty-two more between 1786 and 1790, and 114 between 1791 and 1795. Between 1800 and 1817 the states granted nearly 1800 corporate charters. Massachusetts alone had thirty times more business corporations than the half dozen or so that existed in all of Europe. New York, the fastest growing state, issued 220 corporate charters between 1800 and 1810.

Eventually the pressure to dispense these corporate charters among special interests became so great that some states sought to ease the entire process by establishing general incorporation laws. Instead of requiring special acts of the legislature for each charter specifying the persons, location, and capitalization involved, the legislatures opened up the legal privileges to all who desired them. This destroyed any idea that a corporate grant was an exclusive privilege; instead, it had virtually become a popular entitlement. The states had created hundreds of corporate charters that were considered vested rights of property in the hands of private citizens, not the government.

Turning the charters of corporations into vested rights of private property immune to government tampering was an extraordinary example of the great demarcation brought about by the Revolution. The idea that there existed a sphere of private rights and private property that lay absolutely beyond the authority of the people themselves, was a remarkable innovation: there was virtually no precedents for such an idea in English law or in American colonial experience, except perhaps for the experiments of Roger Williams in Rhode Island and William Penn in Pennsylvania.

Few colonists had ever believed that there were individual rights that could stand against the united will of the community expressed in its representative assemblies. But the Revolution had prepared Americans to accept this innovation in their understanding of individual rights. And it had done so with its radical commitment to the private right of religious freedom. Once Americans were able to limit state authority in religious matters—an area of such importance that no state in history had ever denied itself the power to regulate it—they set in motion the principle that there were some realms of private rights and individual liberties into which executives and legislatures had no business intruding. This was perhaps the greatest of the demarcations of the revolutionary era. If religious corporations earlier created by the state as public entities became private voluntary associations immune from further state tampering, then it was perhaps inevitable that other public corporations came to be treated in a like manner.[37]

There was a curious paradox in this great demarcation. Just as the private vested rights of individuals expanded in these years of the early Republic, so too did the public power of the states and municipal governments. Despite the generous bestowal of corporate charters on multiple private interests, the republican belief that the government should have a distinct and autonomous sphere of public activity remained strong, especially among the new states west of the Appalachian Mountains.[38] Even in the older states many Americans retained a republican faith in the power of government to promote the public good. Those who sought to protect the rights of individuals and private corporations did not deny the public prerogatives of the states. In fact, the heightened concern for the private vested rights of persons was a direct consequence of the enhanced public power the republican Revolution had given to the states and municipalities. Although the power of the federal government certainly declined in the decades following Jefferson's election as president, the public authority, the police powers, and the regulatory rights of the states and their municipalities grew stronger.

Separating the political from the legal, the public from the private, actually allowed for more vigorous state action as long as that action remained within the public realm and served what was called a "public purpose." Individuals may have had rights, but the public had rights as well—rights that grew out of the sovereignty of the state and its legitimate power to police the society. The state of New York, for example, remained deeply involved in the social and economic spheres. Not only did the state government of New York distribute its largess to individual businessmen and groups in the form of bounties, subsidies, stock ownership, loans, corporate grants, and franchises, but it also assumed direct responsibility for some economic activities, including building the Erie Canal.[39]

Even when the states began dissipating their newly acquired public power by reverting to the premodern practice of enlisting private wealth to carry out public ends by issuing increasing numbers of corporate charters, they continued to use their ancient police power to regulate their economies. Between 1780 and 1814 the Massachusetts legislature, for example, enacted a multitude of laws regulating the marketing of a variety of products—everything from lumber, fish, tobacco, and shoes, to butter, bread, nails, and firearms. The states never lost their inherited responsibility for the safety, economy, morality, and health of their societies.[40] The idea of a public good that might override private rights remained alive.

Amidst all this state activity, it was usually left to the courts to sort out and mediate the conflicting claims of public authority and the private rights of individuals. The more the state legislatures enacted statutes to manage and regulate the economy, the more judges found it necessary to exert their authority in order to do justice between individuals and make sense of what was happening. Precisely because of the excessively democratic nature of American politics, the judiciary right from the nation's beginning acquired a special power that it has never lost.

Epilogue

Why didn't Rhode Island attend the Constitutional Convention in 1787? Answering this question might help explain the dynamic way America, or least the northern part of it, developed in the early Republic. In refusing to attend the meeting in Philadelphia, the Rhode Islanders weren't fools. They knew that the Convention was out to change things in ways that would especially harm them. Thus Rhode Island missed the Constitutional Convention, the only state to do so. Not that anyone really cared. The absence of Rhode Island, said one Boston newspaper, was a "joyous" rather than a "grievous" occasion. No one concerned with orderly and virtuous government wanted Rhode Islanders present at the Convention. Because Rhode Island was notorious for its populism and its debtor-inspired paper money emissions, Madison especially disliked it. It was the only state he singled out for condemnation in his memorandum on the "Vices of the Political System of the United States." "Nothing," he said, "can exceed the Wickedness and Folly which continue to rule there. All sense of Character as well as of Right is obliterated there."[1]

Most other leaders agreed with Madison. Rhode Island, they said repeatedly, represented everything that was wrong with the nation in the 1780s, and they called the state every vicious name one could imagine. Rhode Island was a state "verging into anarchy and ruin from democratic licentiousness." Its people were a disgrace to the human race. The state was the continual butt of jokes and poems, such as this from a Connecticut newspaper in 1787: "Hail! realm of rogues, renown'd for fraud and guile, / All hail, ye knav'ries of yon little isle."[2]

Yet, as strange and peculiar as Rhode Island seemed in 1787, the little state anticipated and epitomized developments of nineteenth-century northern middle-class society more trenchantly, more clearly, than other northern states, and for that reason alone its story is worth telling, however briefly.

Rhode Island was a very unusual state and had been a very unusual colony. Overwhelmingly middle-class in character, it anticipated the vibrant capitalistic society of northern antebellum society as no other state did. Quirky from the beginning, it was settled in the seventeenth century by several individuals who are best described as misfits and oddballs. Both Roger Williams, who founded Providence, and Ann Hutchinson, who together with her followers settled in Portsmouth on Aquidneck Island, had been expelled from Massachusetts Bay for their extreme religious views. William Coddington, reputedly the richest merchant in Boston, had come with Hutchinson, but in 1639 he decided to move to the other end of Aquidneck Island, where he founded the town of Newport. Because Coddington had been one of the Puritan judges who had banished Roger Williams from Massachusetts Bay, he and Williams never got along, and he struggled to keep Aquidneck Island, later renamed Rhode Island, separated from Williams and Providence Plantations. Warwick was settled by Samuel Gorton, the oddest of all the colony's founders and a self-educated mystic who preached a theology that no one in New England had ever heard of.

These four towns—Providence, Portsmouth, Newport, and Warwick—with their obstreperous founders and rival patents couldn't get together. A makeshift confederation fell apart in the 1650s and divided into two separate governments with two sets of officials. The royal charter granted by Charles II in 1663 saved the colony from being gobbled up by its neighbors, Massachusetts Bay and Connecticut. The colony's commitment to being a "lively experiment" in religious freedom appealed to the Catholic leanings of the newly restored Stuart king. Partly because of its extreme religious liberty, however, the reputation of the colony remained that of a kind of sewer into which all sorts of cranks and riffraff flowed.

Despite the existence of the royal charter, Rhode Island's towns remained extremely autonomous. So mistrustful of central authority and so jealous of one another were the people of the colony that they had to rotate the capital among the towns. By the eighteenth century the colony had five capitals, one in each county—Newport, Providence, South Kingston, East Greenwich; and the fifth, Bristol, added in 1746.

By the eve of the Revolution Rhode Island had a population of about fifty thousand persons, scarcely a fifth the size of Massachusetts Bay. The extreme localization of authority, the weakness of its social hierarchy, the dominant middling character of its people, and the high percentage of eligible voters made Rhode Island the most democratic colony in the entire British Empire. Between 75 to 80 percent of the adult white males could vote, a higher percentage of eligible voters than any other colony, and surely the highest in the world at that time.

The colony's politics were precocious—anticipating the democratic politics of northern America in the nineteenth century—and unlike the politics of any other colony. In no other North American colony did the people at large directly elect all the officers of the central government. Every April the voters elected on a colonywide basis the governor, the lieutenant governor, the secretary, the attorney general, and the treasurer, together with ten assistants who constituted the upper house of the legislature. For these colony-wide elections, Rhode Islanders developed a peculiar system of party ballots, which they called proxes. For at-large elections, these party proxes were essentially ballots and the only means by which people would know whom to vote for.

The deputies, the representatives in the lower house, were chosen on a local basis. Unlike the non-corporate colonial legislatures, they were elected twice a year, in April and again in August. This Rhode Island assembly was extraordinarily powerful. The April assembly, sitting as committee of the whole, elected for the year the sheriffs, justices of the peace, judges and clerks—that is, all the colonial officers—which in the 1760s numbered more than 250. In nearly all the other colonies, the governors appointed these officials. This is what made Rhode Island's assembly so powerful.

With so much popular participation, the colony's politics took on a raucous volatility that was unmatched anywhere else. The colony was continually racked by something resembling modern party politics. In fact, it was the only colony to develop a modern two-party system, with one faction centered in Providence led by Stephen Hopkins, the other centered in Newport led by Samuel Ward. These political parties were better organized and more modern than any similar factions in the other colonies. To win elections, the parties used every weapon they could, including bribery, name-calling, trickery, corruption, fraud, and lots of rum. Campaign expenses were considerable. In the election of 1763 the Brown brothers of Providence contributed the enormous sum of £1500 to the campaign.

No other colony in North America, probably no other place in the entire world, had this degree of chaotic populist politics. Imperial officials in other colonies shook their heads in bewilderment at what they called a "a downright democracy," where the governor was "a mere nominal one, therefore a cipher, without power or authority, entirely controlled by the populace, elected annually, as all other magistrates and officers whatsoever." In the 1760s the minister of the Congregational Church in Providence labeled this system of politics "Rhode Islandism." "Surer methods," he said, "cannot be taken to ruine a people. . . . For these abominations, our land mourns."[3]

Precisely because its society was so middling-dominated and its elites so weak, the colony became the most commercially advanced of all the colonies in North America. That is, a higher proportion of its people were occupied in buying and selling than anyplace else. The culture of the colony is perhaps best expressed by the Bristol merchant who declared that he "would plow the ocean into pea-porridge to make money."[4]

With all of its ocean harbors, the colony was deeply involved in overseas trade, especially with the West Indies. Ever since the Molasses Act of 1733, designed to protect the rum industry of the British sugar planters in Barbados and Jamaica, smuggling of molasses from the French West Indies became rampant in the colony. Molasses, which was essential to the production of rum, was a by-product of sugar production. Since the French government prohibited its colonial sugar planters in the French West Indies from producing rum, a product France did not want rivaling its wine and brandy industry at home, the Rhode Island merchants were ready buyers for the surplus French West Indian molasses.

Since the Rhode Island merchants had no intention of paying the prohibitory duty on this foreign molasses, smuggling and systematic corruption became a way of life in the colony. The merchants even worked out lists of how much to pay in bribes to the various British customs officials. The rum industry in Rhode Island flourished, with as many as thirty rum distilleries existing in the tiny colony in 1764.

Some 10 percent of the rum that the colony produced was taken to Africa in exchange for slaves who were brought to the Caribbean or to the southern colonies. Rhode Islanders themselves consumed half the rum.

More important than this overseas trade was the domestic trade that Rhode Islanders carried on with each other and with their immediate neighbors. What was crucial for that domestic trade was paper money. Lacking specie—that is, gold and silver, which was to everyone the only real money—the farmers of Rhode Island between 1710 and 1751 pressed the General Assembly to pass no less than nine paper money emissions, flooding New England with paper. A minister in South County named James McSparran explained the unique technique the colony had developed. "Rhode-Islanders," he said, "are perhaps the only People on Earth who have hit upon the Art of enriching themselves by running in Debt."[5]

This paper money, of course, was not good for paying bills in the French West Indies or in London, and consequently merchants in Newport who had overseas creditors deeply resented having to take it. The merchants continually pressed their correspondents and creditors in Britain to put pressure on Parliament to do something about all the paper money in New England. In 1751 Parliament passed a currency act that forbade the New England colonies from making paper money legal tender. But the Rhode Islanders' use of paper money did not stop. Once it became an independent state in 1776, its commercial farmers continued to favor the issuing of paper money.

But in the mid-1780s, during a brief economic downturn, the state's popular passion for paper money outdid itself. In 1786 more voters participated in the spring election than at any time since independence. The so-called Country Party dominated by debtors fearful of losing their farms were overwhelmingly victorious and immediately enacted a radical economic program. The legislature issued £100,000 of legal tender paper money and set penalties for those who refused to accept the paper.

This was too much for Madison and other elites. "Paper Money is still their idol," Madison moaned to Virginia Governor Edmund Randolph in the spring of 1787.[6] Indeed, elite creditors everywhere complained about the excessive paper money being issued by popular state legislatures. Because Rhode Island was the most notorious issuer of paper money, it came to represent all that seemed wrong with American politics in the 1780s. This was why it was the only state Madison expressly criticized in his paper on the "Vices of the Political System of the United States."

Rhode Island and the other states emitting scads of paper money in the 1780s were committing a great injustice, or so it seemed to gentry elites. Debtor majorities in the states were using their majority power to inflict damage on the minorities of creditors who had lent them money. This was striking at the heart of the social order. Unlike the English aristocracy who lived off the rents from long-term tenants, the American gentry elites who constituted whatever aristocracy America possessed had relatively few tenants, land being so much more available in the New World. The American gentry relied instead on the interest earned from money out on loan. In other words, they were creditors lending money to members of their local communities—in effect, acting as bankers in a society that had very few, if any, banks.[7]

In America, as John Witherspoon, president of the College of New Jersey (later Princeton) pointed out in the Continental Congress, rent-producing land could not allow for as stable a source of income as it did in England. In the New World where land was more plentiful and cheaper than it was in the Old World, gentlemen seeking a steady income "would prefer money at interest to purchasing and holding real estate."[8] When merchants and wealthy artisans wanted to establish their status unequivocally as leisured gentlemen, they withdraw from their businesses, and apart from investing in property, they lent their wealth out at interest. Franklin did it. So too did Roger Sherman, John Hancock, and Henry Laurens. It was the way "men of fortune" subsisted, said John Adams. They "live upon their income" from money out on loan.[9]

Consequently, for these gentry creditors, inflation caused by the printing of excessive paper money could be nothing but devastating. For many of them the Constitution was a godsend.

Madison had wanted his new federal Congress to possess a veto over all such unjust debtor-relief legislation enacted by the runaway state assemblies. But he had had to settle for Article I, Section 10 of the Constitution that prohibited the state from doing certain things, including the printing of paper money and making it legal tender. Most gentry welcomed the Section's prohibitions on the states as the righting of a moral and social wrong. In the Virginia ratifying convention Madison told his fellow delegates that paper money was unjust, pernicious, and unconstitutional. It was bad for commerce, it was bad for morality, and it was bad for society. It destroyed "confidence between man and man."[10]

Thus most elite supporters of the Constitution did not see themselves as just another economic interest in a pluralistic society. They were standing up for righteousness itself. "On one side," said Theodore Sedgwick of Massachusetts, "are men of talents, and of integrity, firmly determined to support public justice and private faith, and on the other side there exists as firm a determination to institute tender laws and paper money, . . . in short, to establish iniquity by law."[11]

Many supporters of the Constitution thought that the desire for paper money was the real reason people opposed the Constitution.

"Examine well the characters and circumstances of men who are averse to the new constitution," urged David Ramsay of South Carolina. Many of them turn out to be debtors "who wish to defraud their creditors," and therefore, for some of them at least, Article I, Section 10 of the Constitution may be "the real ground of the opposition." Even Madison thought that many pamphlets opposing the Constitution were omitting "many of the true grounds of opposition." He believed that the articles relating to treaties and "to paper money and contracts, created more enemies than all the errors in the System positive & negative put together."[12]

For those who favored the Constitution, its prohibition of state paper emissions was sufficient reason to support the document. If the new Constitution, said Benjamin Rush, "held forth no other advantages [than] that [of] a future exemption from paper money and tender laws, it would be enough to recommend it to honest men." This was, Rush explained, because "the men of wealth realized once more the safety of his bonds and rents against the inroads of paper money and tender laws."[13]

In the debates over the ratification of the Constitution, the Federalists were able to identify paper money emissions with iniquity and injustice to the point where few dared to justify publicly the printing of paper money. Indeed, the gentry in their writings and speeches, declared William R. Davie in the North Carolina ratifying convention, attached such dishonesty and shame to paper money that even "a member from Rhode Island could not have set his face against such language."[14]

Whether or not paper money could be justified publicly, people undoubtedly wanted it and were determined to get it. The paper money and the debt incurred by people's borrowing of money were not signs of poverty and despair. Far from it, they were signs of progress and intense commercial activity. In fact, if the prohibition on the states' printing of paper money in Article I, Section 10 in the Constitution had been strictly enforced, it would have stifled the economy of the early Republic. The states soon got around the restriction by chartering banks, hundreds of them, that in turn issued the millions of dollars of paper notes that passed as money needed by enterprising middling Americans doing business with one another.

No place in the world had more paper money flying around than did America in the early Republic. By the time the federal government began regulating the money supply in the aftermath of the Civil War, there were more than ten thousand different kinds of notes circulating in the United States.

This proliferation of paper money supplied much of the credit and capital that fueled the extraordinary expansion of the middle-class northern economy of the early Republic. That economy was unbelievably wild and risky, with many failures and bankruptcies; even some states went bankrupt. But success brought great rewards, and ambitious entrepreneurs were everywhere, especially in the norther parts of this rough-and-tumble world; and they needed readily available credit and capital to engage in business. So desirous were people of money that the counterfeiting of bills flourished, with as much as 80 percent of the legitimate bills successfully counterfeited. Criminals fashioned fraudulent copies of the notes issued by the banks and slipped countless amounts of them into circulation alongside the presumably more genuine paper. Storekeepers and businesses often turned a blind eye to the counterfeit bills as long as people were willing to accept them.[15]

Madison and the other founders scarcely comprehended what was happening, and none of them welcomed all the wildcat banks and the helter-skelter economy developing in the North. Even Hamilton, who at least understood how a bank worked, misread the future and was never in control of events. He never really grasped the way the American economy was developing. He and the other Federalists tended to favor big merchants and financiers and to ignore the middling artisans, small businessmen, and commercial farmers. He was confused by the rapid spread of hundreds of state-chartered banks, for he had expected his Bank of the United States (BUS) to create several branches that would eventually absorb the state banks and give the BUS a monopoly of the nation's banking. Moreover, he intended his BUS to make credit available only to large merchants engaged in overseas commerce and to others who wanted short-term loans of ninety days or less. At the outset most Federalist banks, including the BUS, did not want to get involved as yet with long-term mortgage loans to farmers; to do so would tie up money for too long a time. It was the states that created the many banks that ordinary people wanted.

Jefferson had no comprehension whatsoever of what was taking place, especially in the middle-class strata of the North. All Jefferson could see were "banking establishments," which he claimed were "more dangerous than standing armies." They were dangerous because of all the paper money they issued—paper money, he said, that was designed "to enrich swindlers at the expense of the honest and industrious part of the nation." He never grasped how "legerdemain tricks upon paper can produce as solid wealth as hard labor in the earth. It is vain for common sense to urge that *nothing* can produce but *nothing*."[16]

John Adams was as innocent of banking as Jefferson. To the end of his life he was convinced that "every dollar of a bank bill that is issued beyond the quantity of gold and silver in the vaults, represents nothing and is therefore a cheat upon somebody."[17] Of course, the only way a bank could earn any money for its investors was to issue more paper than it had gold or silver in its vaults.

Like other members of the gentry, Adams condemned all the paper money flooding the countryside. He disliked what Rhode Island was doing in the 1780s as much as Madison. "The Cry for Paper Money," he said in 1786, "is downright Wickedness and Dishonesty. Every Man must see that it is the worst Engine of Knavery that ever was invented."[18]

Because Rhode Island was more dominated by middling people than any other state in the Union, it knew what paper money could do, and it had known that for decades. Rhode Islanders were never a poor, backward people sunk in debt. It's true that the recession of 1786 threatened overextended farmers who were able to take advantage of the state's democratic politics with an excessive emission of paper money. But for most Rhode Islanders paper money was capital, and they wanted it now more than ever. It didn't take long for them to realize that they could get around the restrictions imposed by the Constitution by chartering banks. Once they had belatedly joined the Union in 1791, they took the lead in the issuing of paper money, as they had in the colonial period. The Rhode Island legislature went wild in the creating of banks.

By 1819 Rhode Island had thirty-three banks, nearly one in every town. As Pease's *Gazetteer* of 1819 pointed out, "the amount of banking capital here [in Rhode Island] is much greater, in proportion of population, than in any other state." Those banks were spread all over the state, even in agricultural districts; Rhode Island was the only state in the Union, said the *Gazetteer*, to try this "experiment, as to the utility of the general distribution of banks."[19]

Some of the banks issued more paper than was sensible. The Farmers Exchange Bank of Glocester emitted over $600,000 in paper, but had only $86.45 in specie to support these notes. This was too much, even for Rhode Island, and in 1809 the state legislature closed the bank, making it the first bank to go bankrupt in United States history.[20]

All this paper money and the participation of the state's commercially minded middling farmers and artisans in the early nineteenth century prepared the way for Rhode Island's extraordinary commercial success. In the course of the nineteenth century Rhode Island became an economic powerhouse. Inventions flourished, and more patents per capita were issued in Rhode Island than in almost any other place in the English-speaking world.

This extraordinary commercial development, in turn, attracted wave after wave of immigrants from Ireland, Canada, Italy, and elsewhere. By the last part of the nineteenth century, Rhode Island had become a major industrial center. The state dominated manufacturing in textiles, steam engines, baking powder, jewelry, silver, and small tools. Five factories—the Corliss Steam Engine Co., Nicholson File Co., Gorham Manufacturing Co., American Screw Co., and Brown and Sharp Manufacturing Co.—were the largest of their kind, not only in the United States but in the world.[21]

Rhode Island had a flourishing economy, but its politics were as corrupt as ever. Bribery, electoral fraud, and sleaziness were rampant and seemed to have always existed; indeed, at the beginning of the twentieth century "Rhode Islandism" was still being used to characterize the state's politics. Lincoln Steffens, the muckraking journalist, thought that "the political condition of Rhode Island is notorious, acknowledged, and it is shameful." The democratic legislature still dominated. "The General Assembly, corrupt itself," said Steffens, "is a corrupting upper council for every municipality in the State." It was as if nothing had changed in a century's time. But Rhode Island was no longer an outlier, and its peculiar system was just an exaggeration of what was going on elsewhere. Its system had produced Senator Nelson Aldrich, the most powerful political figure in the country and one of the most powerful politicians in the nation's history—"the general manger of the United States," Steffens called him. Just as it had in 1787, Rhode Island had become an object lesson in what progressive reformers needed to change, and, like Madison, they were still yearning for a "dispassionate and disinterested umpire" to set things right.[22]

NOTES

Introduction

1. [Thomas Paine], *Common Sense: Addressed to the Inhabitants of America* (Philadelphia, 1776), in Gordon S. Wood, ed., *The American Revolution: Writings from the Pamphlet Debate, 1764–1776* (New York: Library of America, 2015), 2: 679–80. Of course, Paine, like many Americans, was thoroughly versed in British radical Whig thinking, which often fit the circumstances of the New World better than it did those of the Old World. Bernard Bailyn, *The Ideological Origins of the American Revolution* (Cambridge, MA: Harvard University Press, 1967). Some of Paine's ideas about constitution-making, for example, can be found in James Burgh's three-volume *Political Disquisitions: Or, an Enquiry into Public Errors, Defects, and Abuses* (London, 1774–75). An American edition of Burgh's work was published in Philadelphia in 1774 and endorsed by seventy-five prominent Americans. Oscar Handlin and Mary Handlin, "James Burgh and American Revolutionary Theory," *Proceedings of the Massachusetts Historical Society* 73 (1961): 38–57.
2. John Adams to Benjamin Waterhouse, October 29, 1805, in Gordon S. Wood, ed., *John Adams: Writings from the New Nation, 1784–1826* (New York: Library of America, 2016), 438.
3. Bernard Bailyn, "The *Federalist* Papers," in *To Begin the World Anew: The Genius and Ambiguities of the American Founders* (New York: Knopf, 2005), 100–130.
4. John Adams to William Steuben Smith, May 30, 1815, Adams Family Correspondence, Massachusetts Historical Society; Adams to Jefferson, June 28, 1813, in Lester J. Cappon, ed., *The Adams-Jefferson Letters: The*

Complete Correspondence Between Thomas Jefferson and Abigail and John Adams (Chapel Hill: University of North Carolina Press, 1959), 2: 339; Adams to William Tudor Sr., February 25, 1800, in Gordon S. Wood, ed., *John Adams: Writings from the New Nation, 1784–1826* (New York: Library of America, 2016), 389.

5. Abraham Lincoln, "Speech at Chicago, Illinois, 19 July 1858," in *Abraham Lincoln, Speeches and Writings, 1832–1865*, ed. Don E. Fehrenbacher (New York: Library of America, 1974), 1: 456. For an elaboration of this point about American nationhood, see Gordon S. Wood, "Can the United States Be One People?" in Joshua A. Claybourn, ed., *Our American Story: The Search for a Shared National Narrative* (Lincoln: University of Nebraska Press, 2019), 55–65.

6. Mary Sarah Bilder, *Madison's Hand: Revising the Constitutional Convention* (Cambridge, MA: Harvard University Press, 2015), 1.

7. Pauline Maier, *Ratification: The People Debate the Constitution, 1787–1788* (New York: Simon & Shuster, 2010), 148, 158, 145, 255–56.

8. [Hamilton], *The Federalist*, No. 78.

9. Right from the beginning of professional history writing in the early decades of the twentieth century, James Harvey Robinson and his collaborators emphasized the need for a usable past. They criticized their predecessors for overemphasizing the past at the expense of the present, and they called for a "new history" that could help reform the present. What Robinson and his colleagues wanted was the kind of usable history, an instrumentalist history, that could meet the political and social needs of the present. This was perhaps not an unworthy aim, but it is one that can be easily abused; and it often has been abused, especially in the academic history writing of the present day. See John Harvey Robinson, *The New History: Essays Illustrating the Modern Historical Outlook* (New York: Macmillan, 1922); and John Harvey Robinson and Charles Beard, *The Development of Modern Europe: An Introduction to the Study of Current History* (New York: Ginn & Co., 1907), 1: 1–3.

Chapter 1

1. My account of the imperial debate highlights central issues but is by no means exhaustive. For fuller authoritative accounts of the constitutional issues involved in the imperial relationship, see Jack P. Greene, *The Constitutional Origins of the American Revolution* (Cambridge: Cambridge University Press, 2011); William E. Nelson, *The Common Law in Colonial America*, vol. 4, *Law and Constitution on the Eve of Independence, 1735–1776* (New York: Oxford University Press, 2018); and Craig Yirush, *Settlers, Liberty, and Empire: The Roots of Early American Political Thought, 1675–1775* (New York: Cambridge

University Press, 2011). See also Jack P. Greene and Craig B. Yirush, eds., *Exploring the Bounds of Liberty: Political Writings of Colonial America from the Glorious Revolution to the American Revolution*, 3 vols. (Carmel, IN: Liberty Fund, 2018).

2. Declaration of the Stamp Act Congress, October 19, 1765, in Jack P. Greene, ed., *Colonies to Nation, 1763-1789: A Documentary History of the American Revolution* (New York: Norton, 1975), 64.

3. Declaration of the Stamp Act Congress, October 19, 1765, in Greene, *Colonies to Nation*, 64. One issue that needs further exploration relates to James Otis's presumably archaic notion of law, which allowed him to claim that Parliament's power was absolute but at the same time limited: it could not enact a statute that was unjust. Other Americans made the same point in 1765-66 and appealed to Sir Edward Coke's judgment in Dr. Bonham's case (1610). Otis and others were assuming, in almost medieval terms, that Parliament was still a court and that statutes were not acts of legislative will but court-like judgments that had to be in accord with the principles of the common law to be acceptable. If the statute violated those principles, another court could set the statute aside as null and void. This was not modern judicial review. Coke and Otis simply did not accept the modern notion that law was the enacted will of the legislature. To help understand both Coke and Otis, see Samuel E. Thorne, "The Constitution and the Courts: A Re-Examination of the Famous Case of Dr. Bonham," in Conyers Read, ed., *The Constitution Reconsidered* (New York: Columbia University Press, 1938), 15-24; Bernard Bailyn, ed., *Pamphlets of the American Revolution, 1750-1776* (Cambridge, MA: Harvard University Press, 1965), 1: 100-103, 106-7, 121-23, 409-17, 546-52; and Gordon S. Wood, *The Creation of the American Republic, 1776-1787* (Chapel Hill: University of North Carolina Press, 1969), 262-65. For a South Carolina court's invocation of Coke and Dr. Bonham's case in 1766, see Nelson, *Common Law in Colonial America*, 124-25.

4. [Thomas Whately], *The Regulations Lately Made concerning the Colonies and the Taxes Imposed on Them, Considered* (London, 1765), in Gordon S. Wood, ed., *The American Revolution: Writings from the Pamphlet Debate, 1764-1776* (New York: Library of America, 2015), 1: 236, 239.

5. Some recent American historians have become so used to denigrating America's past in terms of present values that they can't help slipping into anachronism. Alan Taylor, for example, in his big book on American revolutions concludes that because the colonial legislatures denied women, free blacks, and propertyless white males the vote, "colonial America was a poor place to look for democracy." But where else in the world in the mid-eighteenth century was there a better place to look for democracy? Taylor, *American Revolutions: A Continental History, 1750-1804* (New York: Norton, 2016), 36.

6. [Daniel Dulaney], *Considerations on the Propriety of Imposing Taxes in the British Colonies, for the Purpose of Raising a Revenue, by Act of Parliament* (Annapolis, 1765), in Wood, *American Revolution: Writings*, 1: 241–304.

7. [John Joachim Zubly], *An Humble Enquiry into the Nature of the Dependency of the American Colonies upon the Parliament of Great Britain . . .* (Charleston, 1769), in Wood, *American Revolution: Writings*, 1: 589, 602, 593, 591–92.

8. James Otis, *Considerations on Behalf of the Colonists* (London, 1765), 6.

9. Edmund Burke, "Speech to the Electors of Bristol" (1774), in *The Works of the Right Honorable Edmund Burke*, rev. ed. (Boston: Little, Brown, 1865–66), 2: 96.

10. The Declaratory Act (March 18, 1766), in Greene, *Colonies to Nation*, 85. As William Nelson points out, Parliament in the Declaratory Act "announced its view that it possessed power to end local self-government" in the colonies. With the Coercive Acts in 1774 it did just that. Nelson, *Common Law in Colonial America*, 45.

11. William Blackstone, *Commentaries on the Laws of England* (Oxford, 1765–69), 1: 48–49, 160–62, 91. Although J. W. Gough, *Fundamental Law in English Constitutional History* (Oxford: Clarendon Press, 1955), is over six decades old, it is still the best work on the subject.

12. *An Examination of Doctor Benjamin Franklin, Before an August Assembly, relating to the Repeal of the Stamp Act, &c* (1766), in Wood, *American Revolution: Writings*, 1: 141.

13. Townshend, quoted in Lawrence Henry Gipson, *The Coming of the Revolution, 1763–1776* (New York: Harper, 1954), 173.

14. [John Dickinson], *Letters from a Farmer in Pennsylvania, to the Inhabitants of the British Colonies* (1768), in Wood, *American Revolution: Writings*, 1: 444.

15. Bernard Bailyn, *The Ideological Origins of the American Revolution* (Cambridge, MA: Harvard University Press, , rev. ed. 1992), 144–50; Gordon S. Wood, "Conspiracy and the Paranoid Style: Causality and Deceit in the Eighteenth Century," *William and Mary Quarterly* 39 (1982): 401–41.

16. Nelson, *Common Law in Colonial America*, 20.

17. [Allan Ramsay]. *Thoughts on the Origin and Nature of Government* (London, 1769), in Wood, *American Revolution: Writings*, 1: 514–15. In the debate the colonists repeatedly invoked the example of Ireland, often in a confusing manner. See Gordon S. Wood, "The American Revolution and the Use and Abuse of Ireland," in Francis D. Cogliano and Patrick Griffin, eds., *Ireland and America: Empire and Revolution* (Charlottesville: University of Virginia Press, 2021).

18. [William Knox], *The Controversy Between Great Britain and Her Colonies Reviewed* (1769), in Wood, *American Revolution: Writings*, 1: 638.

19. Dickinson, *Letters from a Farmer*, in Wood, *American Revolution: Writings*, 1: 410–11.

20. *The Speeches of His Excellency Governor Hutchinson to the General Assembly . . . with the Answers of His Majesty's Council and the House of Representatives Respectively* (Boston, 1773), in Wood *American Revolution: Writings*, 2: 50, 10.

21. *Speeches of His Excellency Governor Hutchinson. . . with the Answers of . . . the House of Representatives*), in Wood *American Revolution: Writings*, 2: 39.

22. *Speeches of His Excellency Governor Hutchinson. . . with the Answers of . . . the House of Representatives*), in Wood *American Revolution: Writings*, 2: 84.

23. Hutchinson in his March 6, 1773, speech referred to "an anonimous pamphlet" that he claimed had misled the representatives in the House. Presumably this pamphlet was Edward Bancroft's *Remarks on the Controversy Between Great Britain and Her Colonies* (New London, CT, 1771), in Wood, *American Revolution: Writings*, 1: 671-742. Bancroft based his argument on a detailed survey of the origins of the seventeenth-century crown-chartered colonies. He contended that the colonies were distinct states existing outside the realm and thus outside of all parliamentary authority; yet at the same time he concluded that the colonists remained in the British Empire by virtue of their common allegiance to the king.

    Political theorist Eric Nelson claims that Bancroft's pamphlet "became the most influential patriot text of the early 1770s." In his book *The Royalist Revolution* he uses Bancroft's pamphlet to account for the colonists' sudden focus on the king, ignoring the role the problem of sovereignty played in the colonists' total disavowal of Parliament's authority and in their new and exclusive tie to the king. Nelson believes that the colonists were serious and sincere in the early 1770s in wanting a strong and independent Stuart-like king to whom they could tie themselves. His evidence for this astonishing claim, he says, is that "they proceeded to wage a decade-long campaign to realize their Royalist constitutional vision in the new United States," that is, in the strong presidency Americans created in the new Constitution of 1787. But there were many other reasons for Americans to create a strong presidency in 1787, something no American patriot in 1770s could even begin to contemplate. See Eric Nelson, *The Royalist Revolution: Monarchy and the American Founding* (Cambridge, MA: Harvard University Press, 2014), 43, 7, 23, 9, 28; and Gordon S. Wood, "Revolutionary Royalism: A New Paradigm?," *American Political Thought: A Journal of Ideas, Institutions, Culture* 5 (Winter 2016): 132-46.

    In 1775 when the Tory Daniel Leonard made the same claim as Nelson, John Adams in a dazzling display of legal learning emphatically denied that having the colonies tied to the king outside the realm was meant to "build up absolute monarchy in the colonies." Adams, "Novanglus VII, VIII, IX, X, XI, XII," in Gordon S. Wood, ed., *John Adams: Revolutionary Writings, 1755-1783* (New York: Library of America, 2011), 1: 510-30, 536-43, 546-56, 574-83, 588-614, quotation at 540.

24. [James Wilson], *Considerations on the Nature and the Extent of the Legislative Authority of the British Parliament* (Philadelphia, 1774), in Wood, *American Revolution: Writings*, 2: 113. "Allegiance to the King and obedience to Parliament," said Wilson, "are founded on different principles. The former is founded on protection: The latter on representation. An inattention to this difference has produced, I apprehend, much uncertainty and confusion in our ideas concerning the connexion, which ought to subsist between Great Britain and the American Colonies." Wood, *American Revolution: Writings*, 2: 133–34.

25. Lord North, quoted in Nelson, *Royalist Revolution*, 31. Charles McIlwain made the same point in his prize-winning book on the American Revolution written nearly a century ago. "America's final constitutional position was not Whig at all: it was," said McIlwain, "a position in some respects not merely non-Whig, but anti-Whig, for the doctrine of a parliament both omnipotent and imperial against which they were really fighting was more a Whig than a Tory principle." Like Nelson, McIlwain ignores the colonists' problem with sovereignty and instead uses the example of Ireland to mount a legal or constitutional brief on behalf of the American cause, arguing that the American colonies existed from the beginning outside the realm and therefore outside of Parliament's authority. A few years later Robert Livingston Schuyler persuasively demonstrated that McIlwain was wrong. Charles Howard McIlwain, *The American Revolution: A Constitutional Interpretation* (New York: Macmillan, 1923), 159; Robert Livingston Schuyler, *Parliament and the British Empire: Some Constitutional Controversies concerning Imperial Legislative Jurisdiction* (New York: Columbia University Press, 1929), 2, 33, 62, 84–85, 238n.

26. See Randolph G. Adams, *Political Ideas of the American Revolution: Britannic-American Contributions to the Problems of Imperial Organization* (Durham, NC: Trinity College Press, 1922).

27. [Alexander Hamilton], *The Farmer Refuted* (New York, 1777), in Harold C. Syrett and Jacob E. Cooke, eds., *The Papers of Alexander Hamilton* (New York: Columbia University Press, 1961–87), 1: 164; [John Adams], Novanglus, No. VII, March 6, 1775, in Wood, *John Adams: Revolutionary Writings, 1755–1783*, 1: 516.

28. [Wilson], *Considerations on the Nature and the Extent of the Legislative Authority of the British Parliament*, in Wood, *American Revolution: Writings*, 2: 145.

29. Declaration and Resolves of the First Continental Congress, Oct. 14, 1774, in Greene, *Colonies to Nation*, 245.

30. [Thomas Jefferson], *A Summary View of the Rights of British Americans* (Williamsburg, 1774), in Wood, *American Revolution: Writings*, 2: 101, 106–7.

31. [Thomas Paine], *Common Sense: Addressed to the Inhabitants of America* (Philadelphia, 1776), in Wood, *American Revolution: Writings*, 2: 673, 698, 662, 680, 667, 651.

32. Declaration of Independence, in Greene, *Colonies to Nation*, 299, 300.

Chapter 2

1. Declaration of Independence, in Greene, *Colonies to Nation*, 300.
2. Jefferson to Thomas Nelson, May 16, 1776, in Julian P. Boyd et al., eds., *The Papers of Thomas Jefferson* (Princeton, NJ: Princeton University Press, 1950), 1: 292.
3. John Jay, Charge to the Grand Jury, Kingston, New York, September 9, 1777, in Hezekiah Niles, ed., *Principles and Acts of the American Revolution* (Baltimore, 1876), 181.
4. Jefferson to Nelson, May 16, 1776, in *Papers of Jefferson*, 1: 292.
5. Francis Lightfoot Lee to Landon Carter, November 9, 1776, in Paul H. Smith et al., eds., *Letters of the Delegates to Congress, 1774–1789* (Washington, DC: Library of Congress, 1976–2000), 5: 462–63.
6. Adams, *Thoughts on Government, Applicable to the Present State of the American Colonies* (1776), in Gordon S. Wood, ed., *John Adams: Revolutionary Writings, 1755–1783* (New York: Library of America, 2011), 2: 50. Adams had been asked by four or five delegates at the Continental Congress for advice on constitution-making, and after writing several letters by hand he decided to publish his advice as a pamphlet.
7. Adams, Autobiography, in Wood, *John Adams: Revolutionary Writings*, 2: 641.
8. New York constitution (1777), Art. V and Art. XVI. The New York constitution even provided for a census every seven years. All the Revolutionary state constitutions can be conveniently found on the internet in the Avalon Project.
9. [Benjamin Rush], *Observations upon the Present Government of Pennsylvania in Four Letters* (Philadelphia, 1777), in Dagobert D. Runes, ed., *The Selected Writings of Benjamin Rush* (New York: Philosophical Library, 1947), 68.
10. Address of the Massachusetts Convention (1780), in Oscar Handlin and Mary Handlin, eds., *The Popular Sources of Political Authority: Documents on the Massachusetts Constitution of 1780* (Cambridge, MA: Harvard University Press, 1966), 437. Although John Adams had drafted the Massachusetts constitution, this description of the governor as the representative of the whole people was not the product of his words or his intention. He still considered the governor to be the monarchical element in the traditional mixed constitution. His colleagues who wrote the Address after had returned to Europe had moved way beyond that old-fashioned notion of mixed government.
11. William Hooper to NC Congress, October 26, 1776, in William L. Saunders ed., *The Colonial Records of North Carolina* (Raleigh, NC: P. M. Hale, 1886), 1: 867; Jefferson, Third Draft of the Virginia Constitution, in *Papers of Jefferson*, 1: 356; Adams, *Thoughts on Government*, in Wood, *John Adams: Revolutionary Writings*, 2: 52.
12. Jefferson, Third Draft of the Virginia Constitution, in *Papers of Jefferson*, 1: 359.

13. Impeachment as a device for getting rid of obnoxious ministers of the Crown had not been used in England since the early years of the eighteenth century. But in 1774 John Adams, to the amazement of his colleagues, discovered it as a means of intimidating the new royally appointed Massachusetts judges. Following Adams's advice in his *Thoughts on Government*, many of the framers wrote the device into their Revolutionary state constitutions, but confusedly. Some even suggested that members of the legislatures could be impeached. Finding a proper court to try the impeachments, said James Madison, was "among the most puzzling articles of a republican Constitution. . . . The diversified expedients adopted in Constitutions of the several States prove how much the compilers were embarrassed on this subject." Adams, in L. H. Butterfield et al., eds., *Diary and Autobiography of John Adams* (Cambridge, MA: Harvard University Press, 1962), 3: 299–302; Madison's Observations on Jefferson's Draft of a Constitution for Virginia, in *Papers of Jefferson*, 1: 382.

14. Georgia Constitution (1777), Art. XXIV.

15. Richard Henry Lee to Charles Lee, June 29, 1776, in James Curtis Ballagh, ed., *The Letters or Richard Henry Lee* (New York: Macmillan, 1911–14), 1: 203.

16. Lord Bolingbroke, *A Dissertation upon Parties* (1733), quoted in Charles H. McIlwain, *Constitutionalism, Ancient and Modern* (Ithaca, NY: Cornell University Press, 1947), 3. In 1776 Charles Inglis, an Irish-born clergyman who served as Anglican minister of Trinity Church in New York City, in his Tory response to Paine defined a constitution in terms very similar to those of Bolingbroke of four decades earlier. "The constitution—that word so often used—so little understood—so much perverted"—was, said Inglis, "*that assemblage of laws, customs, and institutions which form the general system; according to which the several powers of the state are distributed, and their respective rights are secured to the different members of the community.*" [Charles Inglis], *The True Interest of America, Impartially Stated* (Philadelphia, 1776), in Wood, *American Revolution: Writings*, 2: 721. On the customary constitutions that each of the colonies possessed on the eve of the Revolution, see William E. Nelson, *The Common Law in Colonial America: Law and the Constitution on the Eve of Independence, 1735–1776, Vol. IV* (New York: Oxford University Press, 2018).

17. *The Charge of Judge Paterson to the Jury in the Case of Van Horne's Lessee against Dorrance: Tried at a Circuit Court for the United States, held at Philadelphia, April Term 1795* (Philadelphia, 1796).

18. Thomas Paine, *Rights of Man* (1791), in Philip S. Foner, ed., *The Complete Writings of Thomas Paine* (New York, 1945), 1: 278.

19. James Wilson, in Robert G. McCloskey, ed., *The Works of James Wilson* (Cambridge, MA: Harvard University Press, 1967, 304; Young, quoted in McIlwain, *Constitutionalism*, 1–2.

20. [Moses Mather], *America's Appeal to the Impartial World* (Hartford, 1775), in Wood, *American Revolution: Writings*, 2: 599.

21. William Blackstone, *Commentaries on the Laws of England* (London, 1765–69), 1: 126; William Paley, *The Principles of Moral and Political Philosophy* (Philadelphia, 1788), quoted in Wilson, "Lectures on Law," in McCloskey, *Works of Wilson*, 1: 310; emphasis in original.

22. Adams, *Boston Gazette*, February 8, 1773, in Robert J. Taylor et al., eds., *The Papers of John Adams* (Cambridge, MA: Harvard University Press, 1977–), 1: 292.

23. *The Crisis*, No. XI (New York, 1775), 81–87; Mary Beth Norton, *1774: The Long Year of Revolution* (New York: Knopf, 2020), 125–26.

24. [Samuel Adams], Letter from the House of Representatives of Massachusetts to the Speakers of Other Houses of Representatives, February 11, 1768, in Harry A. Cushing, ed., *The Writings of Samuel Adams* (New York: Putnam's, 1904), 1: 185.

25. [John Joachim Zubly], *An Humble Enquiry into the Nature of the Dependency of the American Colonies upon the Parliament of Great Britain . . .* (Charleston, 1769), in Wood, *American Revolution: Writings*, 1: 585–86.

26. The confusing debates over the nature of written constitutions in the 1770s and 1780s were necessary preludes to the debates in the Congress in the 1790s over imagining and fixing the nature of the federal Constitution that Jonathan Gienapp focuses on brilliantly in his book *The Second Creation: Fixing the American Constitution in the Founding Era* (Cambridge, MA: Harvard University Press, 2018), chs. 1 and 2.

27. William Slade, ed., *Vermont State Papers* (Middlebury, VT: I. W. Copeland, 1823), 288, 449.

28. James Warren to John Adams, June 24, 1783, in Worthington C. Ford, ed., *Warren-Adams Letters* (Boston: Massachusetts Historical Society, 1917), 2: 219.

29. *Providence Gazette*, August 5, 1786, October 21, 1786, quoted in Gordon S. Wood, *The Creation of the American Republic, 1776–1787* (Chapel Hill: University of North Carolina Press, 1969), 404.

30. Jefferson's Drafts of the Virginia Constitution (1776), in *Papers of Jefferson*, 1: 345, 354, 364.

31. Jefferson, A Bill for Establishing Religious Freedom (1779), in *Papers of Jefferson*, 2: 545–46.

32. Jefferson, Proposed Revision of the Virginia Constitution, in *Papers of Jefferson*, 6: 280; Jefferson, *Notes on the State of Virginia*, ed. William Peden (Chapel Hill: University of North Carolina Press, 1955), 121–25

33. Jefferson, *Notes on the State of Virginia*, 123–25.

34. Instructions for Our Representatives, relative to a Constitution, June 11, 1778, in Handlin and Handlin, *Popular Sources of Authority*, 309.

Chapter 3

1. Articles of Confederation, in Greene, *Colonies to Nation*, 128–36. This chapter and the next one are adapted from material in the Charles Edmundson Historical Lectures that I gave at Baylor University in 1987 and published as *The Making of the Constitution* (Waco, TX: Baylor University Press, 1987), and used with permission; all rights reserved.

2. The Confederation Congress was, in fact, a substitute for the king and was granted the powers the former monarch had exercised, which, of course, did not include the authority to tax or to regulate trade. See Jerrilyn Greene Marston, *King and Congress: The Transfer of Political Legitimacy, 1774–1776* (Princeton, NJ: Princeton University Press, 2014).

3. John Fiske, *The Critical Period of American History* (Boston: Houghton, Mifflin, 1888), 55.

4. E. James Ferguson, *The Power of the Purse: A History of American Public Finance, 1776–1790* (Chapel Hill: University of North Carolina Press, 1961), 337.

5. J. Potter, "The Growth of Population in America, 1700–1860," in D. V. Glass and D. E. C. Eversley, eds., *Population in History: Essays in Historical Demography* (Chicago: Aldine, 1965), 640.

6. Charles Thomson to Jefferson, April 6, 1786, in *Papers of Jefferson*, 9: 380.

7. Charleston *South Carolina Gazette and General Advertiser*, August 9, 1783.

8. Merrill Jensen, *The New Nation: A History of the United States, 1783–1789* (New York: Knopf, 1950), 424.

9. Charles Beard, *An Economic Interpretation of the Constitution of the United States* (New York: Macmillan, 1913, 1935), 48; Jackson Turner Main, *The Antifederalists: Critics of the Constitution, 1781–1789* (Chapel Hill: University of North Carolina Press, 1961), 177–78. The title alone of Michael J. Klarman's book, *The Framers' Coup: The Making of the United States Constitution* (New York: Oxford University Press, 2016) suggests a degree of skullduggery on the part of the framers.

10. Address of the Annapolis Convention, September 14, 1786, in Greene, *Colonies to Nation*, 510–11.

11. Washington, quoted in Andrew R. L. Cayton, *The Frontier Republic: Ideology and Politics in the Ohio Country, 1780–1825* (Kent, OH: Kent State University Press, 1986), 23.

12. John Jay, Address Before Congress on Spanish-American Diplomacy, August 3, 1786, in Ruhl J. Bartlett, ed., *The Record of American Diplomacy* (New York: Knopf, 1952), 56.

13. Jefferson to John Adams, November 13, 1787, in Lester J. Cappon, ed., *The Adams-Jefferson Letters: The Complete Correspondence between Thomas Jefferson and Abigail and John Adams* (Chapel Hill: University of North Carolina Press, 1959), 1: 212.

14. Alfred F. Young, *The Democratic Republicans of New York: The Origins, 1763–1797* (Chapel Hill: University of North Carolina Press, 1967), 27.

15. James Madison, Vices of the Political System of the United States (1787), in William T. Hutchinson et al., *The Papers of James Madison* (Chicago: University of Chicago Press, 1962–), 9: 346.

16. Jefferson, Autobiography, in Merrill D. Peterson, ed., *Thomas Jefferson: Writings* (New York: Library of America, 1984), 40.

17. Drew R. McCoy, "The Virginia Port Bill of 1784," *Virginia Magazine of History and Biography* 83 (1975): 294, 292; Madison to Edmund Pendleton, January 9, 1787, to Jefferson, December 4, 1786, in *Papers of Madison*, 9: 244, 191, 225, 200.

18. Madison to George Washington, December 24, 1786, to Edmund Pendleton, January 9, 1787, in *Papers of Madison*, 9: 225, 244.

19. McCoy, "Virginia Port Bill," *Virginia Magazine* 83 (1975): 292; Madison to George Washington, December 7, 1786, to Washington, December 24, 1786, to Edmund Pendleton, January 9, 1787, in *Papers of Madison*, 9: 200, 225, 244.

20. Madison to Jefferson, December 4, 1786, to Washington, December 24, 1786, in *Papers of Madison*, 9: 200, 225.

21. Madison, Vices of the Political System, in *Papers of Madison*, 9: 354–56.

22. John Adams to Richard Cranch, July 4, 1785, in Gordon S. Wood, ed., *John Adams: Writings from the New Nation, 1784–1826* (New York: Library of America, 2016), 54; Washington to Gov. George Clinton, April 20, 1785, to Battaile Muse, December 4, 1785, in W. W. Abbot and Dorothy Twohig et al., eds., *The Papers of George Washington: Confederation Series* (Charlottesville: University of Virginia Press, 1992–97), 2: 510, 3: 431–32; Morris in Mathew Carey, ed., *Debates and Proceedings of the General Assembly of Pennsylvania on the Memorial Praying a Repeal of or Suspension of the Law Annulling the Charter of the Bank* (Philadelphia, 1786), 90.

23. Address of the Council of Censors, February 14, 1786, in William Slade, ed., *Vermont State Papers* (Middlebury, 1823), 540.

24. Louis Otto to Vergennes, French foreign minister, October 10, 1786, in George Bancroft, *History of the Formation of the Constitution of the United States of America* (New York: Appleton, 1892), 2: 399–400.

25. Jerry Grundfest, *George Clymer: Philadelphia Revolutionary, 1739–1813* (New York: Arno Press, 1982), 164–65; E. Wayne Carp, *To Starve the Army at Pleasure: Continental Army Administration and American Political Culture, 1775–1783* (Chapel Hill: University of North Carolina Press, 1984), 209. Washington to Henry Lee, Jr., April 5, 1786, Founders Online.

26. Ezra Stiles, *The United States Elevated to Glory and Honor* (1785), in John Wingate Thornton, ed., *The Pulpit of the American Revolution; or the Political Sermons of the Period of 1776*, Boston: D. Lothrop, 1876), 420.

27. Adams, Novanglus, No. V, in Gordon S. Wood, ed., *John Adams, Revolutionary Writings, 1755–1775* (New York: Library of America, 2011), 1: 473.
28. Jefferson, *Notes on the State of Virginia*, 120.
29. Madison, Vices of the System, in *Papers of Madison*, 9: 345–57.
30. [Noah Webster], "To the Public," May 8, 1787, in Harry R. Warfel, ed., *The Letters of Noah Webster* (New York: Library Publishers, 1953), 64–65; Boston *Independent Chronicle*, May 10, 1787.
31. Higginson to Nathan Dane, June 16, 1787, in J. Franklin Jameson, ed., "Letters of Stephen Higginson," American Historical Association, *Annual Report, 1896*, 1: 759–60.
32. Address of the Annapolis Convention, September 14, 1786, in Greene, *Colonies to Nation*, 510–11.
33. Knox, quoted in William Winslow Crossley and William Jeffrey Jr., *Politics and the Constitution in the History of the United States* (Chicago: University of Chicago Press, 1980), 3: 420–21.
34. Madison, quoted in Charles Warren, *The Making of the Constitution* (Cambridge, MA: Harvard University Press, 1947), 82.

Chapter 4

1. Proceedings of the Confederation Congress, *Journals of the Continental Congress* 32 (February 21, 1787): 73–74.
2. Madison, Notes on Debates, February 21, 1787, in *Papers of Madison*, 9: 291.
3. Editorial note, in *Papers of Jefferson*, 9: 208; [Melancton Smith?], *Letters from the Federal Farmer to the Republicans (1787–88)*, ed. Walter Hartwell Bennett (Tuscaloosa: University of Alabama Press, 1973), 6–7.
4. Benjamin Franklin at eighty-one threw off the average somewhat. Madison was thirty-six, Alexander Hamilton thirty-two, Edmund Randolph thirty-three, and Gouverneur Morris thirty-five.
5. Richard Beeman, *Plain, Honest Men: The Making of the American Constitution* (New York: Random House, 2009), 92
6. Gordon S. Wood, "The Democratization of Mind in the American Revolution," in Robert H. Horwitz, ed., *The Moral Foundations of the American Republic* (Charlottesville: University of Virginia Press, 1986), 122.
7. Randolph, in Max Farrand, *The Records of the Federal Convention of 1787* (New Haven, CT: Yale University Press, 1911, 1937), 1: 41.
8. Madison to Edmund Randolph, April 8, 1787, in *Papers of Madison*, 9: 369–70.
9. Farrand, *Records of the Federal Convention*, 1: 51, 24.
10. Farrand, *Records of the Federal Convention*, 1: 21; Madison to Edmund Randolph, April 8, 1787, in *Papers of Madison*, 9: 369–70.
11. Madison to Washington, April 16, 1787, in *Papers of Madison*, 9: 383–84.

12. Farrand, *Records of the Federal Convention*, 1: 242.
13. Farrand, *Records of the Federal Convention*, 1: 282–93.
14. Martin, quoted by Warren, *Making of the Constitution*, 309.
15. Wilson pointed out that the delegates who wanted equal state representation in the Senate represented states that contained only about one-quarter of America's population. Michael Klarman, *The Framers' Coup: The Making of the United States Constitution* (New York: Oxford University Press, 2016), 201.
16. Farrand, *Records of the Federal Convention*, 2: 18.
17. Madison to Jefferson, September 6, 1787, in *Papers of Jefferson*, 12: 103.
18. On the creation of the electoral college, see Shlome Slonim, "The Electoral College at Philadelphia: The Evolution of an Ad Hoc Congress for the Selection of a President," *The Journal of American History* 73 (1986): 35–58.
19. Madison, *The Federalist*, No. 10.
20. Madison to Jefferson, October 24, 1787, in *Papers of Jefferson*, 12: 276.
21. Madison, *The Federalist*, No. 10. Of the many editions of *The Federalist*, the most authoritative is Jacob E. Cooke, ed., *The Federalist* (Middletown, CT: Wesleyan University Press, 1961). Jay wrote five essays; Madison, presumably twenty-nine; and Hamilton, the rest, fifty-one; there has been contested authorship of some essays.
22. Madison, *The Federalist*, No. 10.
23. Madison to Jefferson, October 24 1787, in *Papers of Jefferson*, 12: 278. For Hume's influence on Madison, see Douglass Adair, "'That Politics May Be Reduced to a Science': David Hume, James Madison and the Tenth *Federalist*," *Huntington Library Quarterly* 20 (1956–57): 343–60.
24. Madison to Jefferson, October 24, 1787, in *Papers of Jefferson*, 12: 275.
25. Madison, *The Federalist*, No. 10.
26. Gordon S. Wood, *The Creation of the American Republic, 1776–1787* (Chapel Hill: University of North Carolina Press, 1969), 514. On the ratification debates in the states, see Pauline Maier, *Ratification: The People Debate the Constitution, 1787–1788* (New York: Simon & Schuster, 2010).
27. Wood, *Creation of the American Republic*, 515.
28. Wood, *Creation of the American Republic*, 516; Singletary, in Merrill Jensen, John P. Kaminski, et al., eds., *Documentary History of the Ratification of the Constitution* (Madison: Wisconsin Historical Society, 1976–), 6: 1231.
29. Smith, in Jensen, Kaminski, et al., *Documentary History of the Ratification of the Constitution*, 22: 1750–51.
30. Wilson, in Jensen, Kaminski, et al., *Documentary History of the Ratification of the Constitution*, 2: 550–51.
31. Pauline Maier, *Ratification: The People Debate the Constitution, 1787–1788* (New York: Simon & Schuster, 2010), 77.
32. Wilson, in Jensen, Kaminski, et al., *Documentary History of the Ratification of the Constitution*, 2: 348, 473, 494.

33. Joel Barlow, *Advice to the Privileged Orders in the Several States of Europe* (1792, 1795) (Ithaca, NY: Cornell University Press, 1956), 17; Harry C. Payne, *The Philosophes and the People* (New Haven, CT: Yale University Press, 1976), 7–17; Fisher Ames, December 1796, *Annals of Congress*, 4th Congress, 2nd session, 1642.

34. Wood, *Creation of the American Republic*, 486.

35. Richard Henry Lee to George Mason, October 1, 1787, in James Curtis Ballagh, ed., *The Letters of Richard Henry Lee* (New York: De Capo Press, 1914), 2: 438.

36. Jefferson to Francis Hopkinson, March 13, 1789, in *Papers of Jefferson*, 14: 650–51.

37. Madison to Jefferson, October 17, 1788, in *Papers of Jefferson*, 14: 20. On Madison, see especially Jack N. Rakove, *A Politician Thinking: The Creative Mind of James Madison* (Norman: University of Oklahoma Press, 2017); and Colleen A. Sheehan, *James Madison and the Spirit of Republican Self-Government* (New York: Cambridge University Press, 2009).

38. Sailors confronted by a whale often threw a tub overboard, hoping to divert the whale's attention. See Kenneth R. Bowling, "'A Tub to the Whale': The Founding Fathers and Adoption of the Federal Bill of Rights," *Journal of the Early Republic* 8 (1988): 223–51.

Chapter 5

1. The literature on slavery in the Revolutionary era is enormous and growing every day. For several different accounts, see David Brion Davis, *The Problem of Slavery in the Age of Revolution, 1770–1823* (New York: Oxford University Press, 1999); Don E. Fehrenbacher, *The Slaveholding Republic: An Account of the United States Government's Relation to Slavery*, ed. Ward M. McAfee (New York: Oxford University Press, 2001); David Waldstreicher, *Slavery's Constitution: From Revolution to Ratification* (New York: Hill and Wang, 2009); George Van Cleve, *A Slaveholders' Union: Slavery, Politics, and Constitution in the Early American Republic* (Chicago: University of Chicago Press, 2019). For a recent study of the initial antislavery movements, see Paul J. Polgar, *Standard-Bearers of Equality: America's First Abolition Movement* (Chapel Hill: University of North Carolina, 2019).

2. Lynn Hunt, *Inventing Human Rights: A History* (New York: Norton, 2007), 207.

3. As David Brion Davis has pointed out, a "French scholar, Raymond Mauny, estimates that between 600 and 1800 as many as fourteen million African slaves were exported to Muslim regions." Davis, *Challenging the Boundaries of Slavery* (Cambridge, MA: Harvard University Press, 2003), 10.

4. John Adams to Robert J. Evans, June 8, 1819, in Gordon S. Wood, ed., *John Adams: Writings from the New Nation, 1784–1826* (New York: Library of America, 2916), 647–48.

5. Marcus W. Jernegan, *Laboring and Dependent Classes in Colonial America, 1807–1783* (Chicago: University of Chicago Press), 55; Richard B. Morris, *Government and Labor in Early America* (New York: Columbia University Press, 1946), 310, 345–63; Jackson Turner Main, *The Social Structure of Revolutionary America* (Princeton, NJ: Princeton University Press, 1965), 33–34; Bernard Bailyn, *Voyagers to the West: A Passage in the People in of America on the Eve of the Revolution* (New York: Knopf, 1986), 292; Cheeseman Abiah Herrick, *White Servitude in Pennsylvania: Indentured and Redemption Labor in Colony and Commonwealth* (Philadelphia: J. J. McVey, 1926), 271; Sharon V. Salinger, *"To Serve Well and Faithfully": Labor and Indentured Servitude in Pennsylvania, 1692–1800* (Cambridge: Cambridge University Press, 1987).

6. Winthrop D. Jordan, *White Over Black: American Attitudes toward the Negro, 1550–1812* (Chapel Hill: University of North Carolina Press, 1968), 3–98; Keith Thomas, *In Pursuit of Civility: Manners and Civilization in Early Modern England* (Waltham, MA: Brandeis University Press, 2018), 173–74.

7. David Galenson, *White Servitude in Colonial America: An Economic Analysis* (Cambridge: Cambridge University Press, 1981), 7–13.

8. Abbot Emerson Smith, *Colonists in Bondage: White Servitude and Convict Labor in America, 1607–1776* (Chapel Hill: University on North Carolina Press, 1947), 265, 276; Morris, *Government and Labor in Early America*, 373, 433, 437, 449, 484.

9. William Eddis, *Letters from America*, ed. Aubrey C. Land (Cambridge, MA: Harvard University Press, 1969), 38;

10. Jack P. Greene, ed., *The Diary of Colonel Landon Carter of Sabine Hall, 1752–1776* (Charlottesville: University of Virginia Press, 1965), 2: 941.

11. Edward M. Riley, ed., *The Journal of John Harrower* (Williamsburg, VA: Colonial Williamsburg, 1963), 38.

12. Herrick, *White Servitude in Pennsylvania*, 272–83; Galenson, *White Servitude in Colonial America*, 231n.

13. Thomas Bacon, *Sermons Addressed to Masters and Servants and Published in the Year 1743, and Now Republished by the Rev. William Meade* (Winchester, VA, [1813]), 3; Pierre Marambaud, *William Byrd of Westover* (Charlottesville: University of Virginia Press, 1971), 169. Although Byrd took his slaveholding for granted, he was no racist. "We all know," he said, "that very bright talents may be lodged under a very dark skin. . . . The principal difference between one people and another proceeds only from the different opportunities of improvement." Richard D. Brown, *Self-Evident Truths: Contesting Equal Rights from the Revolution to the Civil War* (New Haven, CT: Yale University Press, 2017), 108.

14. H. T. Dickinson, *Liberty and Property: Political Ideology in Eighteenth-Century Britain* (London: Weidenfeld and Nicolson, 1977), 89.

15. "The Constitutional Courant" (1765), in Merrill Jensen, ed., *Tracts of the American Revolution, 1763–1776* (Indianapolis: Bobbs-Merrill, 1967), 83; [Stephen Hopkins], *The Rights of the Colonies Examined* (1765), in Wood, *American Revolution: Writings*, 1: 125–26.

16. William Miller, "The Effects of the American Revolution on Indentured Servitude," *Pennsylvania History* 7 (1940): 136; Steven Rosswurm, *Arms, Country, and Class: The Philadelphia Militia and "Lower Sort" during the American Revolution, 1775–1783* (New Brunswick, NJ: Rutgers University Press, 1987), 16.

17. [Samuel Johnson], *Taxation No Tyranny; an Answer to the Resolutions and Address of the American Congress* (London, 1775), in Wood, *American Revolution: Writings*, 2: 496.

18. James Otis, *The Rights of the British Colonies Asserted and Proved* (1764), in Wood, *American Revolution: Writings*, 1: 69–70.

19. Thomas Jefferson, *A Summary View of the Rights of British America* (1774), in Wood, *American Revolution: Writings*, 2: 101–2.

20. James H. Kettner, "Persons or Property? The Pleasants Slaves in Virginia Courts, 1792–1799," in Ronald Hoffman and Peter Albert, eds., *Launching the "Extended Republic": The Federalist Era* (Charlottesville: University of Virginia Press, 1996), 141

21. Alan Taylor, *The Internal Enemy: Slavery and War in Virginia, 1772–1832* (New York: Norton, 2013), 21; Brown, *Self-Evident Truths*, 207–8. Alfred W. Blumrosen and Ruth G. Blumrosen, in *Slave Nation: How Slavery United the Colonies and Sparked the American Revolution* (Naperville, IL: Sourcebooks, Inc., 2005), claim that the Somerset decision had a great influence in the colonies, especially in Virginia, which is given its own chapter. But aside from saying that newspapers printed notices of the decision, they offer no evidence whatsoever that any Virginian slaveholder was actually concerned about the Somerset decision—not one quotation, not one letter from a slaveholder cited. Instead, they use such phrases as "must have taken," "may have been," and "must have heard" to make their case (36, 37). This work has had more influence than it ought to have had.

22. On the Somerset decision, see Van Cleve, *A Slaveholders' Union*, 31–40; and William H. Wiecek, "Somerset: Lord Mansfield and the Legitimacy of Slavery in the Anglo-American World," *University of Chicago Law Review* 42 (1974): 86–146.

23. In the British North American Empire the key protests against the Somerset decision came from West Indian residents in England. See Jack P. Greene and Craig B. Yirush, eds., *Exploring the Bounds of Liberty: Political Writings*

of Colonial America from the Glorious Revolution to the American Revolution (Carmel, IN: Liberty Fund, 2018), 3: 2149.

24. Brown, *Self-Evident Truths*, 108.

25. For a good account of Virginia and slavery in these years, see Eva Sheppard Wolf, *Race and Slavery in the New Nation: Emancipation from the Revolution to Nat Turner's Rebellion* (Baton Rouge: Louisiana State University Press, 2006).

26. Rush to Granville Sharp, November 1, 1774, in John A. Woods, ed., "The Correspondence of Benjamin Rush and Granville Sharp, 1773–1809," *Journal of American Studies* 1 (1967): 13.

27. Washington, quoted in John Richard Alden, *The First South* (Baton Rouge: Louisiana State Press, 1961), 9. Jefferson also thought of the Upper South as different from the Deep South. In his autobiography he listed the "the middle colonies" that hesitated to break from England as "Maryland, Delaware, the Jerseys & N. York." Autobiography, in Peterson, *Jefferson: Writings*, 13.

28. Gary B. Nash, "The African Americans' Revolution," in Edward Gray and Jane Kamensky, eds., *The Oxford Handbook of the American Revolution* (New York: Oxford University Press, 2013), 261. Historians, following the often exaggerated claims of the slaveholding planters, have tended to overestimate the numbers of runaway slaves. See Cassandra Pybus, "Jefferson's Faulty Math: The Question of Slave Defections in the American Revolution," *William and Mary Quarterly* 62 (2005): 243–64.

29. This is the astonishing argument of the 1619 Project of the *New York Times*. The creator of the project, journalist Nikole Hannah-Jones, claims that "one of the primary reasons the colonies decided to declare their independence from Britain was because they wanted to protect the institution of slavery." Apparently, Hannah-Jones, who is seeking justice at the expense of historical truth, believes that Britain in 1776 was on the verge of abolishing slavery and the slave trade, and that prospect forced the colonists to break away from the empire. This project is creating a usable past with a vengeance. *New York Times Magazine*, August 18, 2020.

30. Jefferson, Autobiography, in Peterson, *Jefferson: Writings*, 18.

31. Nelson, *Common Law in Colonial America*, iv, 57–62.

32. An Act to Prohibit the Importation of Negroes into This Colony (1774), in *Records of the Colony of Rhode Island and Providence Plantations*, ed. John Russell Bartlett (Providence, RI: A. C. Greene, 1856–65), 7: 251

33. Vermont Constitution (1777), Declaration of Rights, Art. 1.

34. Pennsylvania, Act for the Gradual Abolition of Slavery (1780), https://en.wikipedia.org/wiki/An-Act-for-the-Gradual-Abolition-of-Slavery.

35. Polgar, *Standard-Bearers of Equality*, 97.

36. *Quack v. Jennison* (1781), *Commonwealth v. Jennison* (1783) www.mass.gov/guide/massachusetts-constitution-and-the-abolition-of-slavery; Michael J.

Klarman, *Framers' Coup: The Making of the United States Constitution* (New York: Oxford University Press, 2016), 260.

37. Northwest Ordinance (1787), Art. VI, in Greene, *Colonies to Nation*, 74.

38. David S. Reynolds, *Abe: Abraham Lincoln in His Times* (New York: Penguin, 2020), 57.

39. Ira Berlin, *Many Thousands Gone: The First Two Centuries of Slavery in North America* (Cambridge, MA: Harvard University Press, 1998), 281; Douglas R. Egerton, *Gabriel's Rebellion: The Virginia Slave Conspiracy of 1802* (Chapel Hill: University of North Carolina Press, 1993), 13.; William G. Thomas III, *A Question of Freedom: The Families Who Challenged Slavery from the Nation's Founding to the Civil War* (New Haven: Yale University Press, 2020).

40. Berlin, *Many Thousands Gone*, 281; John Melish, *Travels through the United States of America in the Years 1806 and 1807, and 1809, 1810, and 1811* (London, 1815), 175.

41. Carl Bridenbaugh, *Seat of Empire: The Political Role of Eighteenth-Century Williamsburg* (Williamsburg, VA: Colonial Williamsburg Foundation, 1950), 10; Higginson to John Adams, August 8, 1785, J. Franklin Jameson, ed., "Letters of Stephen Higginson, 1783–1804," *American Historical Association, Annual Report for 1896* (Washington, DC: Government Printing Office, 1897), 1: 728.

42. Farrand, Records of the *Federal Convention*, 1: 35–36. See the first chapter of James Oakes, *The Crooked Path to Abolition: Abraham Lincoln and the Antislavery Constitution* (New York: Norton, 2020, for a fair-minded account of the slavery issue in the Convention.

43. [Madison], *The Federalist*, No. 54.

44. For a full account of the three-fifths clause, see Van Cleve, *Slaveholders' Union*, 115–42.

45. Farrand, *Records of the Federal Convention*, 3: 420–30.

46. Pauline Maier, *Ratification: The People Debate the Constitution, 1787–1788* (New York: Simon & Schuster, 2010), 284.

47. Farrand, *Records of the Federal Convention*, 2: 364.

48. Dawes, in Jensen, Kaminski et al., *Documentary History of the Ratification of the Constitution*, 6: 1244–45.

49. Klarman, *Framers' Coup*, 295–96.

50. Madison, in Farrand, *Records of the Federal Convention*, 2: 417.

51. Garrison, quoted in Sean Wilentz, *No Property in Man: Slavery and Antislavery at the Nation's Founding* (Cambridge, MA: Harvard University Press, 2018), 12.

52. Reynolds, *Abe*, 148–49.

53. Richard S. Newman, "Prelude to the Gag Rule: Southern Reaction to Antislavery Petitions in the First Congress," *Journal of the Early Republic* 16 (1996): 571–72.

54. Madison to Benjamin Rush, March 20, 1790, in *Papers of Madison*, 13: 109.

55. Stanley Elkins and Eric McKitrick, "A New Meaning for Turner's Frontier: Part II: The Southwest Frontier and New England," *Political Science Quarterly* 69 (1954): 572–76.
56. David P. Geggus, ed., *The Impact of the Haitian Revolution in the Atlantic World* (Columbia: University of South Carolina Press, 2001); Egerton, *Gabriel's Rebellion*, 15.
57. See Gordon S. Wood, "The Revolutionary Origins of the Civil War," *Northwestern University Law School* 114 (2019): 539–53.
58. Reynolds, *Abe*, 777; Brown, *Self-Evident Truths*, ch. 4.
59. Leon F. Litwack, *North of Slavery: The Negro in the Free States* (Chicago: University of Chicago Press, 1961), 75.

Chapter 6

1. Address of the Massachusetts Convention (1780), in Oscar Handlin and Mary Handlin, eds., *Popular Sources of Political Authority: Documents on the Massachusetts Constitution of 1780* (Cambridge, MA: Harvard University Press, 1966), 437. For a comprehensive survey of judicial developments in each of the original colonies, see Scott D. Gerber, *A Distinct Judicial Power: The Origins of an Independent Judiciary, 1606–1787* (New York: Oxford University Press, 2011).
2. [Adams], *Boston Gazette*, January 27, 1766, and Adams, Draft of an Essay on Juries, February 12, 1771, in Wood, *Adams: Revolutionary Writings*, 1: 156–57, 195.
3. [William Henry Drayton], *A Letter from Freeman of South Carolina* (1774), in Wood, *American Revolution: Writings*, 2: 156.
4. [Madison], *The Federalist*, No. 48.
5. Jefferson to Edmund Pendleton, August 26, 1776, in *Papers of Jefferson*, 1: 505. See David Thomas Konig, "Legal Fiction and the Rule of Law: The Jeffersonian Critique of Common Law Adjudication," in Christopher L. Tomlins and Bruce Mann, eds., *The Many Legalities of Early America* (Chapel Hill: University of North Carolina Press, 2001), 97–117.
6. "On the Present State of America," October 10, 1776, in Peter Force, ed., *American Archives*, 5th Series (Washington, DC: M. St. Clair Clarke and P. Force, , 1837–1846), 2: 969; William Henry Drayton, Speech to the General Assembly of South Carolina, January 20, 1778, in Hezekiah Niles, ed., *Principles and Acts of the Revolution in America* (New York: A. S. Barnes, 1876), 359.
7. [Anon.], *Rudiments of Law and Government, Deduced from the Law of Nature* (Charleston, SC, 1783), 35–37.
8. Lynn W. Turner, *William Plumer of New Hampshire, 1759–1850* (Chapel Hill: University of North Carolina Press, 1962), 34–35.

9. *Commonwealth of VA v. Caton and Others* (November 1782), in Peter Call, ed., *Reports of Cases Argued and Decided in the Court of Appeals of Virginia* (Richmond: Robert I. Smith, 1833), 4: 8, 17–18.

10. Richard Spraight to James Iredell, August 12, 1787, in Griffith J. McRee, *Life and Correspondence of James Iredell* (New York: Appleton, 1857–58), 2: 169–70.

11. Madison, Observations on Jefferson's Draft of a Constitution for Virginia (1788), in *Papers of Jefferson*, 6: 315.

12. *Providence Gazette*, May 12, 1787.

13. Hamilton, *The Federalist*, No. 78.

14. Iredell to Richard Spraight, August 26, 1787, in McRee, *Life and Correspondence of Iredell*, 2: 147.

15. Pendleton in *Commonwealth of VA v. Caton and Others* (November 1782), in Call, *Reports of Cases*, 4: 17.

16. Iredell, "To the Public," August 17, 1786, in McRee, *Life of Iredell*, 2: 147.

17. [Madison], "Helvidius No. 2," August 31, 1793, in *Papers of Madison*, 15: 83; [Madison], *The Federalist*, No. 49.

18. [Madison], *The Federalist*, No. 49.

19. Sylvia Snowiss, *Judicial Review and the Law of the Constitution* (New Haven, CT: Yale University Press, 1990), 74.

20. Farrand, *Records of the Federal Convention*, 1: 97, 73.

21. *Annals of the Congress of the United States* (Washington, DC, 1834), 3: 557.

22. 3 Dallas 172–73; 4 Dallas 18–19.

23. [Hamilton], *The Federalist*, No. 83.

24. Randolph, in Farrand, *Records of the Federal Convention*, 2: 144.

25. While judges were working out the character of the Constitution, members of Congress, as Jonathan Gienapp points out, were themselves imagining the nature of the Constitution, as they groped their way toward an understanding of its fixity. William Gienapp, *The Second Creation: Fixing the American Constitution in the Founding Era* (Cambridge, MA: Harvard University Press, 2018). Relating what the politicians were doing in the Congress to what the judges were doing in the courts in creating and recreating the Constitution in the 1790s remains to be explored. But both politicians and judges seem to have mostly agreed in imagining the Constitution, as Gienapp puts it, as "a textual artifact . . . whose content was defined by the language in which it was written" (10).

26. Snowiss, *Judicial Review*, 64.

27. Gerald Gunther, "Judicial Review," in Leonard Levy et al., eds., *Encyclopedia of the American Constitution* (New York: Macmillan, 1986), 1055.

28. *Marbury v. Madison* (1803), in William Cranch, ed., *U.S. Supreme Court Reports* (Washington, 1804), 177.

29. Hamilton, Remarks in the New York Assembly, February 6, 1787, in Harold C. Syrett and Jacob E. Cooke, eds., *The Papers of Alexander Hamilton* (New York: Columbia University Press, 1961–87), 4: 35.

30. John R. Commons et al., eds., *A Documentary History of American Industrial Society* (Cleveland: A. H. Clark Co., 1910-11)), 3: 231–32; Christopher L. Tomlins, *Law, Liberty, and Ideology in the Early American Republic* (Cambridge: Cambridge University Press, 1993), 133.

31. William R. Casto, *The Supreme Court in the Early Republic: The Chief Justiceships of John Jay and Oliver Ellsworth* (Columbia: University of South Carolina Press, 1995), 150, 156–57; Madison, "Report of 1800," January 7, 1800, in *Papers of Madison*, 17: 333.

32. Stephen B. Presser, *Original Misunderstanding: The English, the Americans, and the Dialectic of Federalist Jurisprudence* (Durham, NC: Duke University Press, 1991), 103.

33. Jefferson to Edmund Randolph, August 18, 1799, in *Papers of Jefferson*, 31: 168–70.

34. Jefferson to Randolph, August 18, 1799, in *Papers of Jefferson*, 31: 168–70.

35. Dumas Malone, *Jefferson the President: The First Term, 1801–1805* (Boston: Little, Brown, 1970), 155.

36. *Marbury v. Madison* (1803), in Cranch, *U.S. Supreme Court Reports*, 166–67.

37. Richard E. Ellis, *The Jeffersonian Crisis: Courts, and Politics in the Young Republic* (New York: Oxford University Press, 1971), 179; Michael Les Benedict, "Laissez Faire and Liberty: A Re-Evaluation of the Meaning and Origins of Laissez-Faire Constitutionalism," *Law and History Review* 3 (1985): 323; Andrew Shankman, *Crucible of American Democracy: The Struggle to Fuse Egalitarianism and Capitalism in Jeffersonian Pennsylvania* (Lawrence: University of Kansas Press, 2004), 145.

38. [Alexander Hamilton], *Federalist*, No. 35.

39. Alexis de Tocqueville, *Democracy in America*, ed. Phillips Bradley (New York: Knopf, 1956), 1: 278.

Chapter 7

1. The title of the chapter is taken from the remarkable book by Rafe Blaufarb, *The Great Demarcation: The French Revolution and the Invention of Modern Property* (New York: Oxford University Press, 2016). Blaufarb in a letter to me suggested that the American Revolution in shedding the private ownership of public power seems to have experienced something similar to what took place in the French Revolution. This chapter is my attempt to answer his suggestion.

2. Hendrik Hartog, *Public Property and Private Power: The Corporation of the City of New York in American Law, 1730–1870* (Chapel Hill: University of North Carolina Press, 1983), 60–68.

3. Providence *Gazette*, February 26 1767.

4. William Douglass, *A Summary, Historical and Political, of the First Planting, Progressive Improvements, and Present State of the British Settlements in North America* (Boston, 1749,), 1: 472.

5. Jefferson, quoted in Gordon S. Wood, *Friends Divided: John Adams and Thomas Jefferson* (New York: Penguin, 2017), 199.

6. William Pencak, *America's Burke: The Mind of Thomas Hutchinson* (Washington, DC: University Press of America, 1982), 3–4.

7. Edward M. Cook Jr., *The Father of the Towns: Leadership and Community Structure in Eighteenth-Century New England* (Baltimore: Johns Hopkins University Press, 1976), 101, and esp. ch. 4.

8. Thomas L. Purvis, *Proprietors, Patronage, and Paper Money: Legislative Politics in New Jersey, 1703–1776* (New Brunswick, NJ: Rutgers University Press, 1986).

9. Randolph Klein, *Portrait of an American Family: The Shippens of Pennsylvania across Five Generations* (Philadelphia: University of Pennsylvania Press, 1975), 149; Pencak, *Mind of Thomas Hutchinson*, 4.

10. John Adams, *Defence of the Constitutions of the United States* (1787), in Charles Francis Adams, ed., *The Works of John Adams* (Boston: Little, Brown, 1850–56), 4: 393.

11. Robert E. Brown, *Middle-Class Democracy and the Revolution in Massachusetts, 1691–1780* (Ithaca, NY: Cornell University Press, 1955), 66; David S. Lovejoy, *Rhode Island Politics and the American Revolution, 1760–1776* (Providence, RI: Brown University Press, 1958), 16–17.

12. Clifford K. Shipton, "Jonathan Trumbull," *Sibley's Harvard Graduates: Biographical Sketches of Those Who Attended Harvard College* (Boston, 1950), 8: 269.

13. John Adams to William Tudor, June 1, 1817, in Adams, *Works of John Adams*, 10: 260.

14. Jack P. Greene, ed., *The Diary of Landon Carter of Sabine Hall, 1752–1778* (Charlottesville: University of Virginia Press, 1965), 2: 627

15. Robert J. Taylor, *Western Massachusetts in the Revolution* (Providence, RI: Brown University Press, 1954), 24; Nelson, *Common Law in Colonial America*, iv, 109.

16. Charles S. Sydnor, *Gentlemen Freeholders: Political Practices in Washington's Virginia* (Chapel Hill: University of North Carolina Press, 1952), 63. Probably nothing illustrates the ideal of political leadership in colonial Virginia better than Robert Munford's play, *The Candidates; Or, The Humours of a Virginia Election* (1770), conveniently published in Greene and Yirush, *Exploring the Bounds of Liberty*, 3: 2023–52.

17. Gordon S. Wood, *The Americanization of Benjamin Franklin* (New York: Penguin, 2004), 55–60

18. Gordon S. Wood, *The Creation of the American Republic, 1776–1787* (Chapel Hill: University of North Carolina Press, 1969, 1998), 144–45.

19. Boston *Evening Post,* January 26 1767, December 1, 1766.

20. Jefferson to the New Haven Merchants, July 12, 1801, in *Papers of Jefferson,* 34: 554–58

21. Hartog, *Public Property and Private Power,* 138; Harry N. Scheiber, "Public Rights and the Rule of Law in American Legal History," *California Law Review* 72 (1984): 217–54.

22. Hartog, *Public Property and Private Power,* 155; Harry N. Scheiber, "The Road to *Munn:* Eminent Domain and the Concept of Public Purpose in the State Courts," *Perspectives in American History* 5 (1971): 363.

23. Three-quarters of everything published in America between 1639 and 1800 occurred in the last thirty-five years of that period, from 1765 to the end of the century.

24. [Charles Carroll], "Letters of First Citizen," February 4 ,1773, in Kate Mason Rowland, *The Life of Charles Carroll of Carrollton, 1737–1832* (New York: G. P. Putnam's Sons, 1898), 1: 247, 252.

25. New Hampshire Constitution (1784), Bill of Rights, Art. IX; Mason, First Draft of the Virginia Declaration of Rights [ca. May 26–29, 1776], in Robert A. Rutland, ed., *The Papers of George Mason* (Chapel Hill: University of North Carolina Press, 1970), 1: 277.

26. Stanley N. Katz, "Republicanism and the Laws of Inheritance in the American Revolutionary Era," *Michigan Law Review* 76 (1977): 1–29.

27. Sydnor, *Gentlemen Freeholders,* 63.

28. Story, quoted in Merrill D. Peterson, ed., *Democracy, Liberty, and Property: The State Constitutional Conventions of the 1820s* (Indianapolis: Bobbs-Merrill, 1966), 79–82; *Report of the Proceedings and Debates of the Convention of 1821, Assembled for the Purpose of Amending the Constitution of the State of New York,* ed. Nathan H. Carter et al. (Albany, NY: E. and E. Hosford, 1821), 243; 235. Conceiving of slaves as proprietary property, as sources of independence and status, was one thing; but thinking of them as modern kinds property, as commodities to be bought and sold, was quite another.

29. Aline Austin, *Matthew Lyon: "New Man" of the Democratic Revolution, 1749–1842* (University Park: Pennsylvania State University, 1981), 134. When the Jacksonians came to power in 1828, they reached the ultimate democratic conclusion and turned the eighteenth-century assumption that social and political superiority should coincide on its head. They explained that anyone at all, regardless of his education or social credentials, could hold public office. "Property in office," they said, was the source of "aristocratic" government. Their opponents could only shake their heads in bewilderment

at the Jacksonian claim that nothing—not respectability, not social status—mattered any longer in the holding of public office. Lynn Marshall, "The Strange Stillbirth of the Whig Party," *American Historical Review* 72 (1967): 445–68.

30. North Carolina Constitution (1776) Declaration of Rights, Art. XXIII.

31. *Pennsylvania Packet*, 2, September 10, 1783, 7, August 23, September 25, 1786; Hartog, *Public Property and Private Power*, 90; Johann N. Neem, *Creating a Nation of Joiners: Democracy and Civil Society in Early National Massachusetts* (Cambridge, MA: Harvard University Press, 2008).

32. *Head & Amory v. Providence Insurance Company*, 6 U.S. 2 Cranch 127 (1804).

33. *Terrett v. Taylor*, 13 U.S. 43 (1815).

34. *Trustees of Dartmouth College v. Woodward*, 17 U.S. (4 Wheat.) 518 (1819).

35. Jefferson to William Plumer, July 21, 1816, *The Papers of Jefferson: Retirement Series*, ed. J. Jefferson Looney et al. (Princeton, NJ: Princeton University Press, 2013), 10: 260–61.

36. Oscar Handlin and Mary Flug Handlin, *Commonwealth: A Study of the Role of Government in the American Economy: Massachusetts, 1774–1861* (Cambridge, MA: Harvard University Press, 1947, 1969), 106–33; E. Merrick Dodd, *American Business Corporations until 1860, with Special Reference to Massachusetts* (Cambridge, MA: Harvard University Press, 1954); Ronald E. Seavoy, *The Origins of the American Business Corporation, 1784–1855: Broadening the Concept of Public Service during Industrialization* (Westport, CT: Greenwood Press, 1982); Pauline Maier, "The Revolutionary Origins of the American Corporation," *William and Mary Quarterly* 50 (1993): 68–69.

37. Johann N. Neem, "Politics and the Origins of the Nonprofit Corporation in Massachusetts and New Hampshire, 1780–1820," *Nonprofit and Voluntary Sector Quarterly* 32 (2003): 344–65; Barry Shane, *The Myth of American Individualism: The Protestant Origins of American Political Thought* (Princeton, NJ: Princeton University Press, 1994), 193–240.

38. Sandra F. VanBurkleo, "'The Paws of Banks': The Origins and Significance of Kentucky's Decision to Tax Federal Bankers, 1818–1820," *Journal of the Early Republic* 9 (1989): 480–87; Sandra F. VanBurkleo, "'That Our Pure Republican Principles Might Not Wither': Kentucky's Relief Crisis and the Pursuit of Moral Justice, 1818–1826" (PhD diss., University of Minnesota, 1988), ch. 6.

39. L. Ray Gunn, *The Decline of Authority: Public Economic Policy and Political Development in New York, 1800–1860* (Ithaca, NY: Cornell University Press, 1988).

40. William J. Novak, *The People's Welfare: Law and Regulation in Nineteenth-Century America* (Chapel Hill: University of North Carolina Press, 1996), 15, 88.

Epilogue

1. Boston *Massachusetts Centinel*, May 19, 1787; Madison to Edmund Randolph, April 2, 1787, in *Papers of Madison*, 9: 561–62.
2. William G. McLoughlin, *Rhode Island: A History* (New York: Norton, 1978), 103; Irwin H. Polishook, *Rhode Island and the Union, 1774–1795* (Evanston, IL: Northwestern University Press, 1969), 166–68. The poem's lines come from the *Anarchiad*, a satire on the 1780s composed by the "Connecticut Wits," a group of writers that included John Trumbull and Joel Barlow.
3. D. Kurt Graham, *To Bring Law Home: The Federal Judiciary in Early National Rhode Island* (DeKalb, IL: Northern Illinois University Press, 2010), 20; David S. Lovejoy, *Rhode Island Politics and the American Revolution, 1760–1776* (Providence, RI: Brown University Press, 1958), 29.
4. William G. McLoughlin, *Rhode Island: A History* (New York: Norton, 1978), 62.
5. Edward Field, ed., *State of Rhode Island and Providence Plantations at the End of the Century: A History* (Boston: Mason, 1902), 1: 182
6. Madison to Randolph, April 2, 1787, in *Papers of Madison*, 9: 561–62.
7. See Gordon Wood, "Interests and Disinterestedness in the Making of the Constitution," in *The Idea of America: Reflections on the Birth of the United States* (New York: Penguin, 2011), 162–68.
8. John Witherspoon, "Speech in Congress on Finances," in *The Works of John Witherspoon* (Edinburgh: John Trumbull, 1805), 9: 133–34.
9. Robert A. East, *Business Enterprise in the American Revolutionary Era* (New York: Columbia University Press, 1938), 20–22.
10. Madison, Notes for a Speech Opposing Paper Money, [November 1, 1786?], *Papers of Madison*, 9: 158–59.
11. Sedgwick, quoted in Taylor, *Western Massachusetts*, 166.
12. David Ramsay, "An Address to the Freemen of South Carolina on the Subject of the Federal Constitution" (1787), in Paul Leicester Ford, ed., *Pamphlets on the Constitution of the United States* (Brooklyn: Historical Printing Club, 1888), 379–80; Madison to Jefferson, October 17, 1788, in *Papers of Jefferson*, 14: 18.
13. Benjamin Rush to Jeremy Belknap, February 28, 1788, quoted in John P. Kaminski, "Democracy Run Rampant: Rhode Island in the Confederation," in James Kirby Martin, ed., *The Human Dimension of Nation Making on Colonial and Revolutionary History* (Madison: State Historical Society of Wisconsin, 1976), 267; Rush to Elias Boudinot, July 9, 1788, in L. H. Butterfield, ed., *The Letters of Benjamin Rush* (Princeton, NJ: Princeton University Press, 1951), 1: 471.
14. Farrand, *Records of the Federal Convention*, 2: 310; 3: 350.
15. Reynolds, *Abe*, 658; Stephen Mihm, *A Nation of Counterfeiters: Capitalists, Con Men, and the Making of the United States* (Cambridge, MA: Harvard

University Press, 2007). Mihm argues that all those proliferating bank notes rested on faith. Once a note was accepted, once someone put confidence in a note presented to him, then the note suddenly acquired value. Confidence, he says, was the engine of economic growth. It was "the mysterious sentiment that permitted a country poor in specie but rich in promises to create something from nothing.... At its core," he writes, "capitalism was little more than a confidence game. As long as confidence flourished, even the most far-fetched speculations could get off the ground, wealth would increase, and bank notes—the very pieces of paper that made it all possible—would circulate." Mihm, *Nation of Counterfeiters,* 10, 11.

16. Jefferson to John Taylor, May 28, 1816, to Col. Charles Yancy, January 6, 1816, in J. Jefferson Looney et al., *Papers of Jefferson: Retirement Series* (Princeton, NJ: Princeton University Press, 2004–), 10: 89, 9: 329.

17. John Adams to Abigail Adams, January 9, 1793, in L. H. Butterfield et al., eds., *Adams Family Correspondence* (Cambridge, MA: Harvard University Press, 1963–), 9: 376.

18. John Adams to Richard Cranch, July 4, 1786, in *Adams Family Correspondence,* 7: 240–41.

19. John C. Pease and John M. Niles, *A Gazetteer of the States of Connecticut and Rhode Island* (Hartford, 1819), 314–15. (I owe this citation to Patrick T. Conley.)

20. Jane Kamensky, *The Exchange Artist: A Tale of High-Flying Speculation and America's First Banking Collapse* (New York: Viking Penguin, 2008), 9, 160.

21. *Providence Magazine,* June 24, 1912, January 27, 1915. (I owe these citations to J. Stanley Lemons.)

22. Lincoln Steffens, "Rhode Island: A State for Sale," *McClure's Magazine 24,* no. 4 (Feb. 1905).

INDEX